SOUNDING BRASS

SOUNDING

BRASS

A Curious Musical Partnership

by S.P. Somtow

DIPLODOCUS PRESS
LOS ANGELES • BANGKOK

Sounding Brass
A Curious Musical Partnership

by S.P. Somtow

First Edition
published by Diplodocus Press
Los Angeles • Bangkok

ISBN:
978-1-940999-33-3 hardcover
978-0-9900142-7-0 trade paperback
978-0-9900142-6-3 ebook

0 9 8 7 6 5 4 3 2 1

SOUNDING BRASS

To Bill

"You know, no matter what foolishness we commit,
we cannot kill the greatness that has been there."

— J. William Middendorf, II

I've been conflicted for so long about all this, but now it's
time to explain what it was really all about.
This partnership was unique in the history of music.
Surely it is merely a footnote —
but what a wild footnote!

Thank you for your generosity, your compassion, and your
quirky vision. Forgive me for saying too much, at times.
But this is a history that can't be allowed to die.

A NOTE FROM THE AUTHOR

I write these words in 2018, and all the wild events in this book transpired in the 1970s, extending into the 1980s a bit. I've entertained friends at dinner with some of these stories, and I've been urged to write a memoir about these events for decades. That I am doing so now is really because I've managed to acquire some distance, some objectivity, and I have a clearer idea of just how much effect all this had on my subsequent development as an artist — not just in music but in all the fields of endeavor I've tried my hand at.

But, a lot of time has indeed passed. Some incidents may have merged or diverged or become edited in the memory as the years went by. However, I'm setting all this down *exactly* as I remember it. I can't guarantee to have remembered every name correctly or got every incident in the right order. And yet, as I grow older, those frenetic years seem more vivid, more clear than ever before.

One reason I demurred for so long is that I didn't want to hurt people. But it is a story that *has* to be told. It may just be a curious footnote in the history of music, but it deserves to be in that history somewhere. And after all this time has passed, I also realize now that I'm the one who can tell the story with the *least* amount of hurt. I have no need, for instance, to attack people's political affiliations, or to grind any axes. I can't excuse someone of exploitation without, if I'm honest, copping to some exploitation myself.

However, I'd like to declare right here and now, since I am known for my fiction: this is *not* a work of fiction. It's as true as my memory can allow. And I am a real writer, so this isn't compiled from some ghost-written ramblings into a tape recorder. As these words are all my own, I want to take this opportunity to apologize for anything I may have mis-remembered, or to any who have been angered by what I've written or feels mischaracterized. Truly. This is how I remember it. It's what I live with and it is a relief to talk about it at last.

CONTENTS

Chapter One
An Elevator in Farragut Square

Once upon a time, almost half a century ago, I was a college student in an elevator at an exclusive club in Washington, DC. The elevator was filled with important people — admirals and such — and I was trying to look as inconspicuous as possible, considering I was a long-haired Asian attired in quasi-hippie garb. As the elevator descended, they began discussing the Secretary of the Navy, one J. William Middendorf, the Second.

One of the Very Impressive Persons said, "What do you think of Middendorf's music?"

Another snickered, "Yeah, yeah, his so-called music."

"I heard a rumor," said the first, "that it's all actually composed by some young oriental guy."

The fly on the wall suddenly became conscious that he was being stared at. Glared at, even. I had the distinct impression that there was some kind of joke being made, that I was somehow the subject of the joke, and that I was missing the punchline.

Now that all this time has passed, it is probably safe for me to confess that I was in fact the "young oriental guy" in question; that I was responsible, in one way or another, for the entire musical oeuvre of J. William Middendorf, II, which consisted of seven symphonies, an opera, numerous tone poems, and over a hundred military marches.

If you were to put the worst possible interpretation of the facts, you might well conclude that this extremely wealthy banker-cum-politician had exploited a young music student, made him churn out reams of music, and passed it off as his own; that said student was the compositional equivalent of a prostitute, selling out his talent for a few shekels. You might expound on the hypocrisy of it all, as J. William Middendorf II gathered ringing endorsements from such luminaries as Yehudi Menuhin and Arthur Fiedler, and waved a baton at the Kennedy Center — on one occasion, even, dressed as a bear.

If you had interpreted the facts in this way (as did one Washington reporter, who twisted my tale into an even taller one and published a sort of "exposé" in the paper) you would have missed the real story altogether.

It is indeed true that I wrote the actual notes. It's true that I churned out so many reams of this music, which was so stylistically antithetical to the kind of music I felt I should be writing, that I burned myself out by the age of about twenty-five and had to embark on a completely different career, as a novelist, and as a result, it was twenty years before the muse of music saw fit to reenter my life.

It's true that this lifetime's worth of musical output was presented to the public as being by J. William Middendorf, II, with me being relegated to a footnoted credit as "arranger" once in a while.

Yes, these things are true, but they are not *the truth*.

As always, the truth is a far more complicated animal.

***

Perhaps I should begin by explaining that this is *not* Mozart's *Requiem*. By this I'm not referring to the popular and entirely unhistorical version of the story found in the movie *Amadeus* but the real story, which is that the eccentric Count Franz von Walsegg commissioned Mozart to write it. This count was in the habit of paying well known composers to compose works which he would pass off as his own. He paid very well, and numerous composers profited because he used to have quartet evenings on Tuesdays and Thursdays at his house, often featuring newly minted quartets under his name.

Count von Walsegg's wife was only twenty years old when she died, and the count hired the very best to compose the requiem that would be performed under his name, in her memory.

Mozart of course died before finishing it, and his wife Constanze really needed the money, so she got Mozart's pupil Süssmayr to finish the piece (a number of other composers had a hand in it as well.) She was therefore able to collect the second half of the fee.

A lot of romantic twaddle has enveloped this story, ending up with the fictionalized demonization of Salieri, who had nothing to do with any of this and was far too famous a composer to be bothered by a *pezzonovante* like Wölferl.

However in its essence this is sort of the archetype of such stories. The great, impoverished composer, soon to die, starving in a garret, the wealthy count waving his chequebook. Inevitably, our hero's tragic death follows, perhaps from consumption or suicide.

Bill Middendorf was no Count von Walsegg. But from my teens and well into my late twenties, he did pay me to produce a body of work, not in my own voice (as Mozart would have done) but in the voice of a average composer of the middle romantic period. He did not just write cheques and pass the work off ... it was not that simple. All that I wrote derived in some way from something in his mind ... a vague humming, a dramatic concept, a pretty picture. We agonized for hours in preparation for the creation of this works, with me banging away at the piano until the wee hours. He was passionate. He yearned in the way that true artists yearn. He was generous, not only with money but with gifts of every kind, making it possible for my college years to be spent in great luxury compared to everyone around me, and making it possible for me to work on my own dream projects without starving in a garret — although I *did* in fact spend some time in the basement of a card-carrying member of the Ku Klux Klan.

In those dozen years, in which I produced, under his name, the entire corpus of work of an imaginary nineteenth-century composer, my patron was an ambassador, a banker, the Secretary of the Navy, a banker again, and Ambassador to the Organization of American States. He played important roles in earth-shaking events such as the Cold War, the Southeast Asian conflict, a major bank takeover, and was one of the people who "knew things" — he warned me of a coup that was about to happen in Thailand which no one in Thailand knew about, for instance, and while working on one of his marches at the Army and Navy Club in Washington, he stopped to console a distraught Oliver North, wringing his hands in the lobby in the throes of Iran-Contra.

While riding the whirlwind of politics, world affairs, and high finance, Bill Middendorf also had to contend with a wild family life which encompassed, within the same household, extremes of the most radical 60s liberalism *and* the most rigid Christian fundamentalism. Constantly keeping a precarious balance between the warring sensibilities of his family was the icing on his political cake.

He found release as an artist. Specifically, as a composer.

Only, he wasn't actually a composer. He dreamed a composer's dreams, but had never been able to learn the techniques for making those dreams real. He was good at so many things, but there was this *one* thing he really wanted to lick. So methodically, using what he always referred to as "my lower middle class intellect", he set himself the task of trying to lick it, with the help of an Asian boy who had many issues of his own.

No, he did not exploit me. Rather, we exploited each other, both taking great pains to avoid any appearance of exploitation. We did not produce "great music" together, but we certainly made up for that in quantity ... and it was all viable music that played effectively to the gallery and the groundlings. I tried to give the music intellectual content by sneaking in ironies and jokes, and he tried to coax me into discovering the "big tune" concealed within his humming. It was the union of Mantovani with Schoenberg, and it should have been a marriage made in hell, but somehow, it came off.

I started to write this book because I am afraid that one day someone will take the bones of this story and add to it a different kind of flesh. It could easily be made into a hatchet job, but that would be missing the whole point of it all.

If you delve into it, it becomes something quite profound. It's a story about the human need to want to break boundaries and exceed limitations. It's about dreams and aspirations, and in the end we need to ask questions about the very nature of art and about why we as humans need art in our lives.

It is also the story of two people from vastly divergent cultures, two people who both, perhaps, felt alienated from the people and situations that surrounded them, and who came to share a strangely intimate bond.

I loved, and still love, this man as a father figure, a patron, a passionate devotee of the arts, and the person who kept me on my feet during many hard times. I think I'm the only person who can tell this story without grinding any axes.

So let's begin ...

***

The Hague, the Netherlands, 1970 ...

I was at the Church of St. John and St. Philip on a street called Spuyweg, standing around at the post-morning-service kaffeeklatsch, wolfing down cookies and socializing with churchgoers. I was about 17 years old.

It was a quiet day in the Hague, as most days there are. My father was the Ambassador of Thailand, and I had come home from school in England ... home to rest up for a year before going to university.

I heard a voice, and looked up to see a ruddy-faced man with short, graying hair, a very friendly, direct way of talking. "I'm the American Ambassador," he said. "I hear you're a genius, and I want you to teach me the piano."

CHAPTER TWO
A REMBRANDT ABOVE THE SOFA

How a young Thai musician (or, at the stage, wannabe musician) came to be in the same place at the same time as a American millionaire Nixonite, in an Anglican church in the Netherlands, is one of those inexplicable quirks of fate that has a decidedly novelistic ring to it, and yet it happened.

I can't say much about how J. William Middendorf II came to be standing in that church hall, but I can perhaps explain a little about what I was doing there. I was supposedly having a "gap year" between Eton and university, but it would a gap year that kept getting longer and longer. It was all because of a conflict between words and music.

When I was about four years old, my father was doing something or other at the International Court of Justice in the Hague; previously, from just after birth, I'd been living in Oxford as my father was doing his doctorate; subsequently I lived in Boston, Massachusetts while my father pursued another degree at Harvard; Holland was the third country I lived in before turning seven.

For some reason, it was decided that I should have piano lessons.

It was not a good idea. My teacher wanted me to play scales and silly songs with three notes in them. I wanted to play the things I could hear in my head. My teacher said, "Why don't you write down one of these little pieces, young man?" I wrote down something with a key signature of six flats. She didn't believe it was really me, and we had tantrums at each other; she fled the house weeping.

Confession: I didn't really know what six flats meant, but I thought it was cool-looking.

At seven or so we went back to Thailand where I spent a bizarrely alienated childhood, at first unable to speak any Thai. Music became a secret passion, along with the ancient Greeks. So by the time I arrived at Eton at the age of 13, I was very mixed up indeed.

It was a rule in those days that everyone on arrival had to have a singing audition, and I hit the jackpot; assigned to sing alto in the Brahms Requiem, real music lessons from top teachers, membership in the prestigious Eton College Chapel Choir, trips to Glyndebourne, committee member of the Eton College Musical Society, — music was my salvation at this school which was a strange junction of Dickensian horror and enlightened 1960s liberal education.

By the time I finished at Eton, my Dad had been made ambassador of Thailand to the Netherlands. Since I had lived there as a child, Holland felt very much like home. The language even started coming back to me.

It was assumed by everyone that I would go to Oxford, that music would be at best an avocation, and that if I was too stupid to read law at my father's old college, English Literature might be an acceptable alternative.

I came "home" to the Netherlands to bone up for an interview at Oxford where everyone assumed I would go in a year or so.

But music continued to speak to me ... and to be my inner voice of salvation....
        ***

I looked for a place where I could continue to listen to that inner voice, and it was only natural to make for the nearest Anglican church. I knocked on the door, and the vicar, one John Lewis, invited me to audition for the choirmaster, one Chris Farr. Since I was, not to put too fine a point on it, at a somewhat higher level of professional training than anyone else in that choir, Chris Farr took me right away and Sundays became my refuge from an increasing reluctance to go to Oxford.

A strange place to end up for a young Thai Buddhist child (and while there's a significant Christian minority in Thailand, few are Anglicans.) But this, indeed, is how I ended up being addressed by no less a figure than the American ambassador, and how I ended up making the 15 minute walk from my father's house on Laan Copes van Cattenburch to No. 4, Tobias Asserlaan, the residence of the U.S. Ambassador.

I found this picture on the internet. I may be wrong but I don't remember a metal fence. I recall being able to walk straight up to the house from the street, without any security of any kind, unthinkable, perhaps, for such a residence today. I wonder whether this house is still the ambassadorial residence.

Ambassador Middendorf came to the door himself, and led me, past a sweeping staircase with a curve in it, to an impressive living room. Above the sofa hung a real Rembrandt.

My memory isn't what it used to me but I seem to remember an inner living room as well, just as hugely proportioned and the whole furnished in a style I think of as "traditional" American. But it was the real Rembrandt that dominated. That, and the grand piano.

My entire image of what the American political élite must be like had been based on seeing pictures of the Kennedys, but nothing could be more different. There was an assortment of kids: the oldest was the dreamy-eyed Frances, the youngest an adorable five-year-old named Ralph, who I believe would one day rechristen himself Roxy.

They ran around underfoot, they quarreled, they were down-to-earth; it was a family I could envy because my father's ambassadorial residence was quite different in tone; it was formal, with a large staff of servants and a complex hierarchy. The mistress of the household was a prim, trim lady named Isabelle who was clearly in charge. She eyed me a bit oddly as I entered the living room, but soon, I think, dismissed the piano lessons as some husbandly eccentricity, and I was left alone with the ambassador, under the glowering gaze of the Rembrandt.

To be honest, I don't recall which Rembrandt it was, but later I heard that he had three, which were from time to time on loan to the Metropolitan or the Rijksmuseum.

"So, Somtow," he said, "the piano. Let's start."

Like any good teacher, I started with C major scales.

Getting the thumb over to finish the scale proved a bit awkward. "I think maybe it's beyond my lower middle class mind," he said — a phrase he used often, and which I can never hear so see in print without having his voice attached to it.

Amazingly, it took around five hours to master the C major scale. And Bill was determined. He was persistent. He wouldn't take "no" from his body, trying over and over to get that thumb over.

When it came to doing it with his left hand, he was a lot happier playing the scale in the reverse direction. By dinnertime, he was happily using both hands in inverse motion, and wondering when he'd get to play an actual melody.

At length he said, "Boy, I'm famished," and he led me to the kitchen (this was a vast kitchen unlike any I had ever seen), where he rooted around and finally produced, triumphantly, two cans of corned beef hash.

We spent the next hour on the sofa, eating corned beef hash out of tin cans, under the watchful eye of a real Rembrandt ... a surreal tableau that has haunted me all my life.

He showed me a picture of a stained glass window he had made for the English church where I had met him. A lovely pastoral scene with a lamb at its center. I was impressed. "You actually made this yourself?"

"Well, I drew it, and had someone do it up in stained glass," he said.

Words which, I was later to learn, summarized his entire world-view when it came to the creative process.

After dinner, he played the C major scale for two more hours. Backwards and forwards and with a childlike excitement and a solemn concentration that I found fascinating. I had never seen someone this old be so engrossed in the details of so seemingly-simple a thing.

It was really late (to my mind) and I had become really tired, but Bill Middendorf seemed to just be getting his second wind. He now tried playing the scale in a new way; rather than crossing his thumb, he turned his entire hand over and played the last three notes with the backs of his fingers in one smooth motion. We had a huge laugh over this.

I imagined myself dining out for years to come on the story of my day of teaching the C major scale to an American diplomat.

You can therefore imagine my surprise when the last thing he said to me, as I left the house that evening, was "Same time tomorrow?"

He then gave me a traveller's cheque for $20, which was the first professional fee I had ever received in my life.

In 1970, $20 was a *lot* of money.

For a 17-year-old, anyway.

CHAPTER THREE
AN EPIPHANY ON A LOAF

I was, you understand, in a gap year. I had all the time in the world. Bill Middendorf, on the other hand, had an ambassadorial career plus some huge business dealings. Not to mention a gaggle of kids and a deeply religious wife — just how religious I was gradually to discover.

How he could pursue the grueling schedule of being a diplomat *and* devote hours each day to a few scales was a mystery to me at first, but it soon became just the way things were.

My gap year was about to become much longer than a year, and much more devoid of academics, because I went up to Oxford for the interview, and was an ignominious failure.

I was already in deep trouble because in the entrance exam, I had committed the unforgivable offence of lampooning Tennyson. You see, there was this poem we had to analyze, and I didn't like it. Indeed, I thought it quite appropriate to say so.

It was only almost half a century later that I learned from my brilliant teacher at Eton, Michael Meredith (who was still there when I visited the school in the early years of the 21st century) what pandemonium my exam answers had caused, and that the choice of text had actually been a trick, as it was a poem Tennyson himself had rejected and withdrawn. Apparently I was the only one taking the exam who had had the chutzpah to see through the ruse. Apparently, irate phone calls had gone back and forth and my housemaster, the infamous "Dippy" Simpson, who had made my life miserable for years, basically told them they shouldn't take me because I was an arrogant little prick.

They weren't predisposed to like me, but I was innocent of all this as I rode up to Oxford in the train in the company of no less a figure than Mom Rajawongse Sukhumbhand Paribatra, a distant cousin of mine and direct descendant of King Rama IV.

He has been telling this story at parties for decades, and basically it goes like this: "They asked Somtow why he wanted to go Oxford, and he answered, 'Well, actually, I was hoping to go to Cambridge.' So they kicked him out and *I* got in."

He also got to be the governor of Bangkok and was implicated in a number of corruption scandals, but I happen to think he was innocent of everything except failing to keep an eye on his underlings. But that's for another book.

The bottom line is that I was no longer going to Oxford, and would be forced to apply again in a year — doubling the length of my gap year. My family were not at all happy to discover that I wanted to go to Cambridge — *and* — the horror — to do music there — and that I intended to compete in the annual choral scholarship tests.

"They will never admit an Asian as a choral scholar," my father told me. "It is simply beyond the realm of possibility." I don't like being told something is impossible merely because of my ethnicity, so I became even more determined, signing up for special music coaching, taking a job playing the piano for a ballet teacher every weekend for 25 guilders a pop, and going to a weekly madrigal sight-reading party hosted in the town of Maasluis by the late David Bolton, who was later to become a fine harpsichord maker.

Still hoping that I'd come to my senses, reapply to Oxford and do something sensible like a law degree, they decided to humour me for a while.

I found myself with almost two years to kill, and a lot of time for music.

Music and *Middendorf.*
***

After the third or fourth C major scale marathon (we never quite managed another key, nor indeed, a minor scale) a few weeks later I found myself under the Rembrandt again.

But before we could start this time, Bill Middendorf said, "Let's take a break. You must help me bake some bread. I'm taking breadmaking *and* music at the same time." We did not have the word *multitasking* in the 1970.

And we retired once more to the cavernous kitchen where a dapper man with a French name, Pierre, and the accent to go with it, was rolling dough. Soon we were all standing around rolling dough and it was quite exciting for a very insulated boy who had never spent much time in kitchens.

Presently we were told that a loaf was done and it was ceremoniously brought out and displayed. "Yours, Mr. Ambassador," said Pierre.

The bread was sliced and we each prepared to chow down, with as much solemnity as if it had been the Holy Eucharist. But Bill said, with great sadness, "I added too much salt." His ruefulness imbued the over-salted bread with a curious sense of tragedy. And soon the ambassador had gone back to the living room.

The bread was indeed, extremely salty, but as the beneficiary of a classical education, I knew that the ancient Romans used to dip their bread in salt, so rather than wrinkling my nose I was rather enjoying it, fantasizing about being in a scene from *Ben Hur.* Miklos Rozsa's heavenly *Love Theme* was ringing in my consciousness when I started to notice an odd kind of counterpoint.

A melody was coming from the living room — and it was in C major — but it wasn't the same old scale. It was being repeated over and over, each time with greater assuredness.

The final three notes, the dotted rhythm returning back up to the tonic, would later turn out to be a major feature of the Middendorf melodic style.

Bill Middendorf was picking this melody out with one finger, over and over, with a great sense of excitement.

"It's something I can kind of hear in my mind," he said. "Something I heard once, a long time ago, only not exactly ... it's like I added an extra something to it. Boy!"

Another element of the Middendorf compositional process was presenting itself, though I didn't realize it at the time, because of course if you take away the middle bar of the three bars, you get the opening of Schubert's C major symphony. And later, many would say, "Middendorf doesn't so much *compose* themes as he *misremembers* them."

"You know, that's very pretty, I said," and I sat down myself and began improvising great cascading arpeggios and big chords around this melody.

Bill Middendorf's hefty frame shook with glee. "That's *it!*" he said. "That's *just* what I meant to say."

I played around with the theme a bit, but it didn't actually go anywhere. "I think it needs a middle bit, sort of a touch of evil," he said. "Can you play something like that?"

I did, blending the original Middendorf melody with a touch of *Parsifal* — the chromatic notes of the wizard Klingsor. "Yes, yes!" he said excitedly.

I said, "I guess we go back to the calm beginning after that. And we have your basic ABA structure."

"I don't know what that means," he said, "but this is what might lower middle class mind hears — the wind on the Zuider Zee. A raging storm. Then the water grows calm."

All this from three bars played with one finger!

"Write it up," he said. "Come back tomorrow."

***

And I did, with about 3 pages of hand-written piano music under my arm. I sat down and played it. Bill Middendorf was transfixed. To me, it may have been a few meandering chord progressions and a few technical tricks woven together into a pseudo-romantic display, but in his eyes I *could* see the play of light on the Zuider Zee, the wind billowing, everything he had talked about the previous night.

Johnny — that is to say, J. William John Middendorf, IV, had wandered into the room. "This is what your Dad wrote," I said to him.

With the deflationary disdain that only a twelve-year-old can muster, he said, "Nuh uh. *You* did."

The bubble burst ... but not for long.

Bill said, "I want a march ... and to close, a waltz. I'm going to call in *Waltz of the Windmills.*"

And he began to hammer out another brief melodic fragment. I started to play things on the piano, pausing at every *"That's it!"* to make a quick note in my manuscript book. By about 2 am, the *Waltz of the Windmills* had come rolling off the assembly line, but the ambassador had graduated from bashing it out with one finger to humming.

Humming made it a lot simpler for me to improvise something, as well. Humming is inherently more vague than hitting precise notes and as the evening wore on, my interpretation of Bill Middendorf's source material became somewhat looser.

After less than a week, we had a three movement sonata, and I had uttered some "famous last words" which unknowingly mapped out about a fifteen years of my future. I said, "You know, I could try orchestrating this."

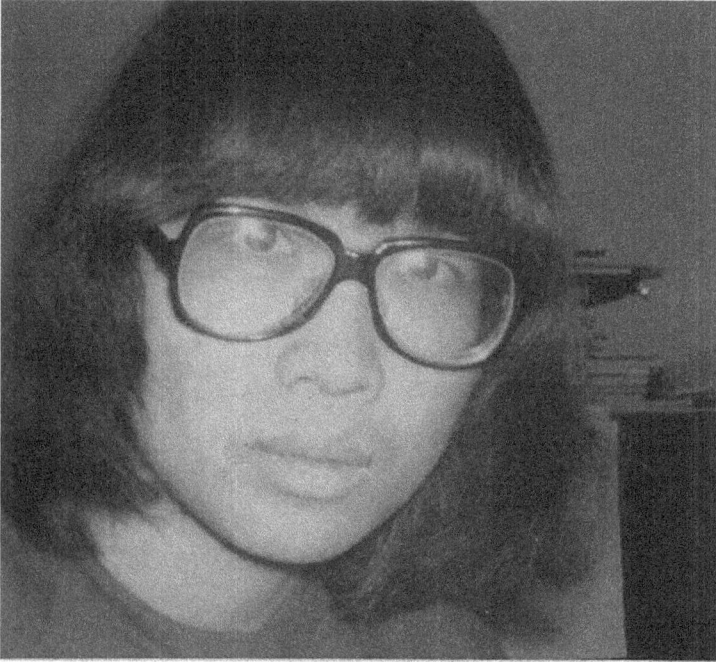

Somtow in the 1970s

Chapter Four
A Sonata with a Minister

He had had Artur Rubinstein to an impressive dinner; Rubinstein had, much to Bill's annoyance, refused to play afterwards. saying that his contract only allowed him to use a Steinway. By now it was clear that J. William Middendorf, II, would never become another Artur Rubinstein.

Still, becoming a composer was a pretty decent consolation prize, especially with someone else doing the heavy lifting.

And shortly thereafter, there was another posh dinner at the ambassador's residence. I was not invited to the dinner, but I *was* the designated postcoenal entertainment.

The entertainment consisted of me, playing Middendorf's *Sonata No. 1 — The Holland Sonata* on the piano. It began with a brief pre-concert lecture in which Bill described with incredible vividness the beautiful scenes of Holland that the music evoked for him: the tulip fields, the storm on the Zuider Zee, the dance of the wooden clogs — it sounded like the ultimate tourist guide to the Netherlands. Then I played.

Now, this sonata was by no stretch of the imagination a masterpiece. It had some nice tunes, tenuously strung together (sometimes with the musical equivalent of chicken wire) and I also have to admit that I didn't stick to the written notes. That's because I'm not really a pianist, and sometimes I just like to go off script a bit.

But the audience was enthralled. After all, here was a distinguished diplomat putting into music his love for the country to which he had been posted. As the person who actually put this to paper, I was all too aware of the trite bits and a few ironic bits —

Among the guests there was one who was being deferred to by all. This was, I learned, Dr. Joseph Luns, who had by then been the Dutch Foreign Minister for about eighteen years, under seven or eight prime ministers. He was just about as famous a Dutchman as you could get in 1971, and he had an urbane wit quite different from the aw-shucks aura that Bill Middendorf projected.

Though in a sense, I was the star attraction of the evening, I was just a teenage kid with long hair. None of the distinguished guests talked to me except to — a little patronisingly perhaps — compliment my interpretation of this fabulous sonata. Only Dr. Luns paid me any attention. In a quiet moment, he asked me directly, "The ambassador really composed this all by himself?"

"Well ... maybe ... I helped a little."

Dr. Luns gave a wry smile, but Bill rescued me from my quandary about how much I should reveal about this ... let's call it unorthodox, for now ... compositional process. With great enthusiasm, the ambassador said, "Why, the boy's a genius. He's helped me a *lot*. He *arranged* the whole thing."

Thus it was that I acquired an "official" status in the musical canon of J. William Middendorf, the Second. I was the *arranger*.

***

The real purpose of the posh dinner became apparent a few days later, when Bill reminded me that I'd said something about *orchestrating* the sonata. "It could be more than a sonata ... it could be a symphony," I said, with just one more movement.

"Yes, opening with a march!" he said excitedly. "My favorite composer is John Phillip Sousa."

He described to me how a march could go. First, trumpet calls in the distance. Then a brilliant, bright military bang-up with clashing cymbals. Then a hymn. Pious, reverent, the deep protestant roots of Dutch culture. Then a dark moment. The Nazi invasion of Holland. Then a battle scene, and finally, a triumphant return of the hymn with bells pealing ... the return of Queen Wilhelmina from exile and the rebuilding of the nation.

It was a stunning scenario. "Of course," Bill said, "It'll need a few themes. Can you do up something?"

He began humming the march to me. Yes, it sounded like Sousa, a *lot* like Sousa, but with a few missing or added notes. His excitement was infectious and soon I was banging out this march on the piano.

"The Queen is going to be tickled pink," he said.

That was when I realized that the sumptuous dinner and the conversation with Dr. Joseph Luns hadn't just been some kind of social pleasantry.

It had been an audition. Bill Middendorf's music was being vetted by important members of the Dutch government, because it was about to have a very high-profile debut, and they had to be absolutely certain that the music would pass muster.

The "Holland Symphony" — improvised by a schoolboy on the piano from five-finger exercises and humming — was about to be presented to Queen Juliana of the Netherlands.

***

What, exactly, *is* an *arranger?* It's a credit you often see on Hollywood motion pictures, school editions of classical music, or song books. An arranger takes a piece of music, and basically turns it into another piece of music.

Mostly commonly, arrangers take a written piece such as something originally composed for piano, and turns it into an orchestral score. Or, in film scoring, takes music that has been fully sketched out by the main composer as to the harmonies, the melodic lines, and fleshes it out with instruments. The point of *arrangement,* is that what the arranger produces is recognizably the same piece as the original, generally with the same inner melodies and harmonies.   In classical arranging, the result is unmistakably the same piece of music as the original.

Or, the arranger's job could move in a more creative direction — he could take a melody and redress it in different harmonies and colors completely, but the melody would still be clearly the original melody.   This usually happens when the source material is folkloric, like a traditional dance tune, or perhaps doesn't even come with harmonies at all.

The further away you get from this, the closer you move toward the realm of actually composing. Vaughan Williams's *Greensleeves Fantasy* is clearly a piece of music composed by Vaughan Williams, even though the traditional melody sounds all the way through it.   At the most extreme end you'd have something like Mahler's *First Symphony,* in which *Frère Jacques* is used in its entirety, yet this not an arrangement at all — it's an ironic reference.

Had I in fact "arranged" the Holland Symphony, or had I simply "composed" the entire thing? This is by no means an easy question to answer, and for the entirety of my involvement in the creation of the Middendorf *oeuvre,* it would be a question fraught with emotional baggage.   I would be tormented by this question for the next dozen years.

The identity crisis was not yet to be precipitated, however. We were still a long way from there.
***

Meanwhile, my musical existence was being greatly enhanced by this new association. As a person with a special relationship with the U.S. Ambassador, I came to the attention of many Americans including, for instance, the very dedicated music teacher at the local American school in the Hague, one Rita Liebermann-Ranucci. I had first met her at one of those madrigal evenings run by David Bolton in Maasluis. She was a competent alto but a really proficient sight-reader, making her absolutely invaluable to the group.

She introduced me to the institution of school music making, American-style, which was quite different from music-making at Eton.

At Eton there was a certain ambition involved in music-making. The school orchestra, which was far to advanced for me to get into, played real symphonies and concertos and accompanied a huge oratorio every few months. Even the "second" orchestra, in which I had been vouchsafed the opportunity to play percussion, played real music — one of my most treasured memories is playing the tam-tam in the Mussorgsky-Ravel *Great Gate of Kiev*. When I asked if I could get a copy of the music, my conductor said, "You don't need it. Just give that thing a hefty thwack at the beginning of every bar until it ends."

In the American School of the Hague, there was music-making as well, but it was a lot more egalitarian. Rita knew how to play pretty much every instrument, and the kids rotated from violin to clarinet without much ado. The repertoire consisted of such immortal classics as *Lightly Row.*

Still, I wasn't a whole lot older than them, and it was fun to hang out. One time, I was called in to be the only cellist in Beethoven's Ninth Symphony — not the whole thing, just "the" tune. I do not know and did not ever played the cello, but she showed me the principles in five minutes, and I found that I could more or less guess where the fingers should go for such a simple tune. Afterwards, she berated me for using vibrato. "You can't have *one* person resonating while the rest of the orchestra is just scratching and squeaking," she said, laughing.

The end result of this was that I ended up knowing a few young musicians (and would-be musicians) — they had parents and friends as well, and soon there was a very uneven chamber orchestra on call, and they would soon have their debut ... in the living room of J. William Middendorf, II.

For, while I was working on orchestrating the grand *Holland Symphony,* (or *Symphonie Hollandaise* as one of my friends jokingly called it) the music lessons continued.

The hymn that formed so crucial a part of the symphony now resurfaced again. The reason it existed at all was that I had been trying to explain four-part harmony to Bill and I had run through a few Bach chorales — which soon ended up as an interesting Lutheran pastiche — the hymn of the pious Dutch according to symphony's programme notes.

While "arranging" the hymn, I would frequently show Bill how this melody could actually be played in all sorts of different styles — and he had the idea that all these versions to be assembled into a sort of —

"Theme and Variations?" I suggested.

"Yes! That's it!"

Before the ink was dry on the symphony, there was already a second opus, a *Concerto for Strings* which had a classical first movement in the *galant* style — at its best, it was almost as brilliant as Salieri on an off day — and then this astonishing "Theme and Variations" which begins with classical music and ends up with a few minutes of pseudo-Mahler, even echoing a climax from the slow finale of the Ninth Symphony (though normalizing the one aberrant note in the Mahler melody, the one note that actually makes it so special).

And in short order I had to conduct a hodgepodge group of students, parents and their friends in a house concert chez Middendorf. Each was receiving the princely sum of $20 (paid, as usual, via travellers' cheques) — and for high school students this was definitely a small fortune.

The concert featured works by Bill Middendorf and, to quote Peter Schickele, "I couldn't help slipping in a little something of my own."

The little something of my own was an intermezzo from an opera about Michelangelo that I was composing on the side. It was not tuneful. Indeed it was decidedly avant-garde, and the audience at the dinner concert barely tolerated it. But after the Mahlerian climax of the string concerto, an ancient viola player who had joined the orchestra murmured, *"Maar dat was heel mooi"* — "but that was really beautiful."

The thing is that the opera I was writing was in what I felt was my true voice. Looking at the score now, it's a bit of a kitchen sink and it began in the world of Schönberg and ended in the world of Penderecki, must as my own exposure to contemporary music had expanded during the time I was composing it. Like a sponge, I was sucking in everything I listened to, and wringing it back out again.

With the Middendorf scores, I was not writing in my own voice. I was trying to get into the thought process of a middle aged white American who adored romanticism.

This is why when young Johnny Middendorf accused me of composing this music myself, an accusation all the members of the family would make at one point or another, my feelings were ambivalent.

I had to tell myself that this was not *my* music. *My* music was something quite different — "lofty", I supposed, "elevated" and decidedly *not* "romantic."

And yet, the *Holland Symphony* was the first time I was able to compose for orchestra ... and actually have it played back by real human beings. Each time I was to create one of these romantic concoctions, I was receiving valuable lessons at a time when no software existed for instant playback, when the *only* way to learn if something "worked" was to just write it and have it played.

***

A curious interlude amid all this occurred one afternoon when I was at the Middendorf house. I was sitting around in the back somewhere and Bill Middendorf came to get me. "There's a bunch of hippies in the living room," he said, "it's a rock group or something."

His daughter Frances was in the hall and rolled her eyes when she heard this. As I passed by she said softly, "It's the *Grateful Dead,* Somtow!"

Bill was performing the ambassadorial function of welcoming visiting celebrities from the homeland, but American culture of the 1970s was not his thing.

He could tell a Rembrandt from a Hals just by winking at it, but he didn't have a clue who Jerry Garcia was. I, who was awestruck, said nothing.

After they left, Frances Middendorf did say a thing or two about how incredible they were, these icons of the counterculture, but her father wasn't buying it. "They've got long hair," he snorted. "They're *hippies.*"

Frances rolled her eyes again (she had a very fetching way of doing so) and said, "But Somtow has long hair."

"Yes," he said, "but it's different. His genius *justifies* his long hair."

***

I was not greeted with equal enthusiasm by the Middendorfs. Isabelle had become increasingly irritated by how much music was consuming Bill's life. She and her daughter Amy were the evangelicals in the group, and I hoped that by mentioning Jesus from time to time, I'd stay on her good side.

Frances, the oldest, was I think the most like her father; she loved the arts, was flamboyant and decidedly *not* evangelical.   Her relationship with her father was not idyllic but I feel that to some extent it was because she was able to be all the things he longed to be himself. I always had the feeling she was his favorite.

There was another daughter named Martha, who mostly ignored me. I've mentioned John, who was twelve, who did have a penchant for telling the truth at the wrong moment.   I don't think he had any feelings about me one way or the other, but he struck me as being rather sensible. Years later, I learned, he climbed mountains, lived in a tent in the wilderness and did other "manly" things — he always struck me as being profoundly grounded. To do that kind of climbing, you have to see things for what they are.

The youngest, Ralph, was sweet and affectionate. Bill once whispered to me, "He likes to be cuddled," mentioning it as a kind of weakness rather a natural thing in a five year old. He's called "Roxy Paine" now and he's an innovative artist. But even at five, he was dreamy, he had a rich inner life.

The invasion of this household by a long-haired Asian teenager was definitely an upheaval, especially since the music sessions were growing longer and longer.

And weirder, too. Lasting well into the wee hours — luckily, the Hague was a perfectly safe place to walk around in in the middle of the night, and lucky, too, that my parents saw nothing bizarre about their teenage son spending so much time tickling the ivories with a grown ambassador.

There were more house concerts as well.   There was a piano concerto performed by David Bolton.

David improvised his own cadenza, which was as long as the rest of the concerto put together. I think Bill was a big perplexed at the cadenza because he didn't remember composing it. Later, a recording was made with a different pianist, on the Phillips label, with a much shorter cadenza.

The piano concerto would later be one of the glories of the Middendorf oeuvre. Each year, at St Catharine's College, Cambridge, the music director Peter Le Huray, would play the recording to all the first year musicians. They would be required to guess the composer.

The guesses were always outlandish.

Finally, Le Huray would proffer a clue. "All I can say," he said, is that there are 'Thais' with Cambridge."

I've given myself away now, because earlier I told you how my father had absolutely refused to believe that any Asian could ever dream of getting a choral scholarship to Cambridge.

So, off-topic for a moment, I did take a break from the Middendorfian world and, to everyone's surprise. successfully passed that audition.

Apparently, I did so when I chose an obscure church sonnet by Frescobaldi as my solo piece. At the close of the piece, I did a "goat trill" — an ornament used in music of the late Renaissance-early Baroque that had only just started to be talked about by early music experts. It was, in fact, this goal trill that did the trick.

The aforementioned Peter Le Huray caught me as I was walking back to the temporary lodgings — I think they were in Trinity College. "How did you know?" he said excitedly. "About the trill."

"Oh, I've been following early music a lot lately."

"Somtow, I see that St. Catharine's College isn't on your list," (one could only select three Cambridge Colleges to apply to, so naturally, believing I was doomed to failure, I had picked King's, St John's and Trinity, the three most famous) "but perhaps you wouldn't mind going to a smaller college? I mean, Cambridge is Cambridge."

My heart almost stopped beating. "Would I mind?" I stuttered. "And ... the academic requirements?"

"Oh, that, he said. Your A level results are fine. Just say yes."

Knowing one piece of trivia about early baroque music had changed my life. I was about to become the first Asian to break the "yellow ceiling" of the British choral world....

Back to the Middendorfs....
***

My self confidence had increased tremendously since that short trip to England, though I had only been able to accept the choral scholarship (well, technically it was an 'exhibition' not a scholarship) after I promised my parents I wouldn't actually go for a degree in music. So English Literature it was to be, on a choral scholarship, but I wouldn't be forced to take a fiendish entrance exam on Shakespeare, Chaucer, or anyone else.

I wrote a "rock" setting of the Anglican mass for John Lewis's church. Some of the gang that played regularly at the Middendorf house concerts were roped in to play, and my sister Kiki got to sing the *Gloria* segment.

John Lewis averred that we could get a lot of attention by doing the "rock mass" at the Middendorf home — at a private service.   The reverend had recently got religion — it's difficult to explain since he presumably must have had it in the first place, in order to become a vicar — but he apparently received a second dose from a wave of pentecostals who were becoming more and more influential.

Mrs. Middendorf was one, so we all presumed that she'd be delighted to have such an uplifting event in her home.   I undertook to ask Bill's permission, and he gave it right away.

The Evangelische Omroep or EO, a Dutch Evangelical TV station, who were doing a documentary about the American diplomat with Jesus in his heart, offered to film the whole thing.   We started rehearsing.

The entire thing was stopped in its tracks when I received a mysterious call from a man who identified himself as Mr. Middendorf's social secretary. Later I was to learn there were two of them, and they had a sort of good cop-bad cop role to play in managing his schedule.

"The rock mass is off," he told me.

"Why?" I said.

"I can't tell you."

"But the ambassador just gave his permission."

There was a long silence.

"You have to understand, Somtow," said the man (whose name I have forgotten, but he was very lean, with a wisp of white hair) "that it's Mrs. Middendorf who has the final say on these matters."

I hadn't noticed this before, so completely consumed had I been in Bill Middendorf's inner world.

I learned later she had had all she could take of her husband's music obsession. She had put her foot down. "I'm not having that thing in my house," she had said.

And the social secretaries knew, it seems, who had the power to make their lives miserable.

However, my disappointment had to be shelved, because we now received word that Queen Juliana of the Netherlands had accepted the dedication of the Holland Symphony. It would be performed in honour of the 25th anniversary of her reign.

"She's having us to tea," the ambassador told me. Then, looking me over and noting that I was wearing green velvet bell-bottoms and a scruffy teeshirt, he added, "You do have a suit, don't you?"

Original LP cover of the "Holland Symphony" on the pretigious Philips label

Chapter Five
A Tea-break with a Queen

The journey to see the Queen of the Netherlands — I was to have two meals with her during the course of my parents' posting in the Low Countries — was a spectacle.

I had never done the police escort thing before. That was exciting. I had met a Queen before, but I had no memory of it.

When I was four years old, during a previous sojourn in Holland, I had been chosen to present flowers to Queen Elizabeth II when she visited our school, the British School of the Hague. Apparently the photo is really cute. I've been trying to find a copy for at least fifty years.

With police motorcycles and flashing lights, the ambassadorial car fairly flew; it was quite far from the Hague so I think it must have been Soestdijk Palace, which has now been sold and is becoming a hotel, so perhaps I'll be able to there and spend the night.

It was a splendid, palace which today you can visit for five Euros. But in those days, it was very much an official residence.

Queen Juliana was famous for being very down-to-earth, frequently riding a bicycle to open Parliament and hoping onto public transportation once in a while.

Of my first meeting with the Queen I remember virtually nothing, because I was too overawed by the whole experience. I did visit her again a year later, however, and that time I remember everything, so we will save it for that moment in this story.

The main thing is that at this tea, Ambassador Middendorf and I were alone with the Queen and he told her he had composed *The Holland Symphony,* and that it would be dedicated to her. She was charmed as he told her how the symphony captured his love of the Netherlands. Now and then, she smiled at me in a lovely, grandmotherly way, especially when Bill waxed fulsomely about my "genius" — an appellation by no means borne out by the work at hand.

Later, he was to reiterate this dedication in front of cameras, and he was very generous to me in his statement. As I recall, perhaps a bit paraphrased: "I had a great deal of help in composing this work from the son of the Thai ambassador, Somtow Sucharitkul, so in a real sense, this is gift to you from the United States ... *and Thailand.*"

Bill Middendorf's magnanimity and inclusiveness on this and so many other occasions was remarkable. There was no real reason to bring me to the tea at all, especially since I was "only" the arranger. Yet he always thought of me.

On this occasion, the tea was brief and I was too awestruck to speak much. I did notice a breach of protocol, however ... after about an hour, Bill Middendorf said to the Queen, "Well, Your Majesty, I guess it's time for us to leave."

As a boy strictly brought up with royal etiquette, I knew that one always waits for a monarch to dismiss one, and never the other way round.

Her Majesty raised an eyebrow.

I have to admit that I was more shocked than she was. She wasn't very big on formality. I was happy enough not to have to back out of the room.

***

The next thing that happened was the the Evangelische Omroep, the religious TV station I mentioned earlier, agreed to broadcast a performance of the symphony for the Queen's 25th Jubilee celebration.

At Bill's insistence, and I think over the dead bodies of numerous studio executives, I was going to get to conduct this premiere.

I think they were worried at first that I would blow it and that it would be safer to have a real conductor.   Later on, they concluded that if a teenaged Asian boy were to do this, even ineptly, it would add a certain charm to the video. It could even be a selling point.

The technology of it all was amazing to me. First, we were going to make an audio recording of the symphony.

Then, they would play it back and the entire orchestra would *pretend* to play, in a completely different setting, while I pretended to conduct.

But talk about the deep end.

Today, I have a battery of machines in my office. I type in notes and they play back — with the actual sounds of the instruments involved.   If I write something for orchestra, it plays back with every note sounding very close to how it would sound if played by a rather inhumanly in-tune orchestra conducted by a mechanical but competent conductor.

In 1971, the procedure was all in the mind. I had to imagine what it sound like if this instrument played that note and how it would blend or clash with another instrument playing another note. To test out what my imagination created, I had to get an actual orchestra to play.

Naturally, when I stood in front of the orchestra of people all twice or three times my age, attempting not to appear too intimidated, I couldn't very well say, "Whoops, I think that second oboe E flat should really be an octave higher, I'll just rewrite it now...."

In fact, I was going to have to brazen it out.

Generally speaking, it sounded pretty much the way I thought it would, but I was no Mozart. I wasn't really a prodigy — I had turned 18 by now and this was my *first* orchestral attempt. Being casually called a genius at every turn was not that helpful.

Furthermore, I had never had any formal instruction in conducting at that time, which in a way was a blessing because I would have died of embarrassment had I known then what I know now.

I had *been* conducted a lot in school, and by top musicians — Eton has always been known as a musical hub, even in the earliest times (the Eton Choir Book, a carefully preserved manuscript from the time of Henry VIII and the dissolution of the monasteries, is the *only* surviving source of the works of many great English composers.) I had been exposed to a whole lot of brilliance in my school. I'd even conducted one of my own compositions at a school concert, performed by my friends such as (now) world famous countertenor and CBE Michael Chance, who in those days was a flautist.

I also conducted our house choir in a number from *Carmina Burana,* and won first prize, only to be disqualified because of an "unwritten" rule produced at the last minute that competition entries were not allowed to have conductors. This was perhaps a political thing. My housemaster, "Dippy" Simpson, didn't like it when we enjoyed music too much.

And then there were those house concerts in the living room of Ambassador Middendorf.

With this world-shaking résumé and list of credits, I was now unleashed upon 80 very professional and very skeptical Dutchmen, to conduct a work by an amateur composer that had been ghost-written by me.

Being a sublimely overconfident teenager and having been imbued with a full quota of the Etonian sense of entitlement, I didn't get embarrassed until about thirty years later.

So —it was as if, having only ridden a bicycle in my life, I was now being forced to compete in Formula One.

After a couple of abortive upbeats, I managed to acquit myself without too many disasters. But Bill Middendorf was over the moon — I'd never seen him be so excited.

There were only a few incidents that would haunt me a little; one was that I the recording engineer kept noticing a bizarre "mistake" in the first bassoon part … the bassoon had a long leading tone, B to C, while the cellos and basses had a long held C.

It had been a bit of careless orchestration on my part; the bassoon, doubling the melody an octave lower, had precipitated an awkward (and amateurish) clash.

The engineer kept stopping the tape to get a new take of the bassoonist playing the "right" note, only he was just playing what was written.

Later, the same bassoonist demanded a proper cut off at a place where one wasn't written into the score.

In both cases I had to stand by a stupid error that I had made, or look even stupider.

Despite all this ... my deflowering as an orchestral conductor had gone off with few hitches. Next came the "play-acting" art which was in a gorgeous room in some kind of palace. I remember the baroque trimmings of the room (or maybe they were rococo) — a perfect setting for a performance, say, of the Brandenburg Concertos.

For this extravaganza, Bill had ordered me a complete rental set of tails, so complicated to wear that I needed help to get into it. Feeling a little weirded out through the entire operation, I tried to put all the energy and drama at my disposal into the act of looking like a great conductor. I pretended it was Wagner.

Not that difficult, since in at least one spot, I'd referenced *Parsifal* rather too clearly.

The final film, which played on the Queen's jubilee, on the EO channel, was amazing. It was probably just as well they didn't show the conductor very much, but the director had really gone to town. Every bit of the music's "programme" was illustrated. From the U.S. soldiers parachuting down to Queen Wilhelmina's triumphant return to Holland in jerky old newsreel footage, to the gorgeous scenery of sea and tulip and windmill and the Dutch peasants dancing in the rollicking final "Klompendans" number this was long-form MV making, twenty years ahead of Michael Jackson's *Thriller!*

Bill Middendorf's concept, delightful in its naïveté, had been enlarged by me and converted into a not-very-daring nineteenth-century symphony, then dressed up with images and made into an extremely creditable 21-minute film. And the clip in which Bill Middendorf made his presentation of the dedication to the Queen and generously mentioned me as often as he mentioned himself, was beautiful.

The entire package was a superb example of packaging. Some might say it was a silk purse from a sow's ear, but that would be unnecessarily cruel. It was in fact utterly charming. A Dutch magazine summed up the ambassador's achievement: "He wrote the entire symphony after only a few months' coaching — and that at the hands of a student!"

Bill Middendorf was hooked.

"When can we start on the next symphony?" he asked me.

The next symphony was going to be *epic*. For I was about to be introduced to one of J. William Middendorf, II's most enduring passions — the Crusades.

Recording session for the Holland Symphony

Chapter Six
A Brush with Religion

I had entered the world of professional music making through a side door. But having somehow managed to sneak inside, I was determined to gain a foothold. But how?

My mind was certainly not focused on creating fake nineteenth-century symphonies. Indeed at that time in my life, the mainstream of romanticism, Bill Middendorf's favorite stomping ground, was about as far from my own taste as you could get.

I had arrived in Holland after finishing at Eton with an enduring love of opera, especially the late romantic works of Strauss. My taste in orchestral music started around Wagner and went to the mid-twentieth century, and backwards from Beethoven to

Mozart. There was a gaping hole in my taste which happened to be the very hole in which Bill Middendorf loved most to dwell — the middle of the nineteenth century.

But taking frequent trips to nearby London, only an hour away by plane, to see old school friends, take the Oxford exam and the Cambridge exam, and see concerts had exposed me to earlier and earlier genres of music and by the middle of 1971 I'd acquired a big obsession with mediaeval music, collecting all the LPs by Musica Reservata and going to their concerts. Thus it was that I stumbled on a melody composed by Richard the Lionheart, *ja nun hons pris.*

One day at the Middendorf house, I started to play this melody on the piano, accompanying it with some bare fifths in typical mediaeval style. The ambassador was entranced.

"What is it?" he asked. When I told him, he said, "You mean it's authentic music from the Crusades?" His eyes just lit up. I came to realize that the Crusades were an important part of his inner fantasy life.

"Do you know any other music from then?"

I couldn't think of anything Crusades-specific, but I said, "Well, the monks used to sing these ancient hymns like *Pange lingua.*" I played it to him (all in fifths, in the *organum* style, which made it sound very mediaeval.)

I told him about the early music concerts I had been to in London, and about musical instruments like rebecs and crumhorns and nakers. Each exotic instrument name was amazing to him. It was like Christmas!

"We've gotta use them all in a symphony," he said.

In vain I protested that it was unlikely that rebecs could be heard against a huge symphony orchestra, but that was not going to stop Bill Middendorf from bringing a new vision to life.

He said, "Listen. There's these monks, chanting as they march toward Jerusalem. There's Richard the Lionheart leading his knights. There's this soaring love theme that comes from Richard's own music. Then there's Saladin. The saracens, with weird, Arabic-sounding music. A battle scene. And then —"

"A triumphal march?" I asked him.

"No." He shook his head. "Our heroes lose Jerusalem. Chanting the same old chant, they slowly march back to Europe."

The way he told the story was profoundly personal. As if, almost, he had been there in person.

I whipped out my notepad and prepared for a full night of improvising "Arabic-sounding" music.

***

It turned out that Bill Middendorf was a lot more knowledgeable about the Crusades than he appeared (or wanted you to think.) He didn't *actually* believe that Saladin was a barbarous Arab; he actually did realize that he was a somewhat educated Kurd. He also knew that Richard the Lionhearted had a bit of sexual ambiguity.

The Crusades of his fantasy had more in common with Hollywood than the Middle East. And the score that came to life from his humming and my banging bore a great resemblance to my favorite epic movie composer, Miklos Rozsa, creator of the scores of *Ben Hur, Quo Vadis, El Cid* ... I guess we'll stop at *Dead Men Don't Wear Plaid.* They bore this resemblance for the simple reason that the Rozsa sound was my go-to style when imagining "epic" in my head. True, too, of Bill Middendorf, even though he may not have consciously realized who composed which movie scores.

Parts for rebecs, recorders, and viols were added to the symphony — many of these early instruments didn't come from the same century, but a bit of anachronism wasn't bothering anyone.

Getting this huge work performed would have to wait a while, but in the succeeding months two more symphonies poured from our collaborative pen.

I remember almost nothing about No. 3, which I think was a lighter, chamber work; but No. 4 was quite ambitious. It had a Mahlerian finale not unlike that of the finale of Mahler 5 — indeed it was a sort of *Reader's Digest* version of that famous movement.

***

Meanwhile, the brouhaha over performing the *Rock Mass* in the Middendorf household was leading me toward a rather curious byway in my life, my brief flirtation with the pentecostals.

I said earlier that the vicar of the local Anglican church had recently experienced a dramatic religious awakening. As a result, this normally staid and *very* English church had been invaded by a lot of new blood. After I had composed the *Rock Mass,* much of it inspired by such luminaries as John Lennon, some of this "new blood" decided to join the performance.

Here's the thing, though, I'm not absolutely sure I remember their names. I think maybe this is an episode that I've partially blocked from my memory. But I'll call them Dean and Michelle as these are the names that come to mind; they might even be their real names.

Both of them were fine musicians and singers and I welcomed them. But at the end of one rehearsal, Michelle said to me, "I can't go on unless you tell me the answer to this question. Are you saved?"

Despite being the winner of the Brinkman Divinity Prize at Eton for submitting a 100-page essay titled *Memoirs of Ahab,* I had no idea at first that she was even talking about religion.

I had composed this mass because after five years of singing in choirs, the Anglican choral tradition was in my blood and these were great words to set to pretty tunes. I had not composed the music out of belief in one specific deity, let alone one specific vision of that deity. So I had no idea what she was talking about.

But she invited me to a gathering at Dean's apartment, and I had few friends. So I went. It was a very pleasant thing, and with my background in comparative religion (remember, I won a divinity prize in school!) I got along well with them, could match them quote for quote, even though I found their earnestness a little unnerving.

It occurred to me, however, that these people were members of a continuum which included Isabelle Middendorf. I had already figured out that I needed her not to be my enemy.

Isabelle Middendorf

These people, to my surprise, believed that they possessed superpowers — the ability to prophesy, for instance, or to speak in tongues, or to translate the words of someone else who had just spoken in tongues — and more scientifically problematic superpowers such as the ability to heal.

After dinner, they started tonguing up a storm. I couldn't help but notice that when they spoke in tongues, they rarely went outside the phonemic range

of the regular languages that they already spoke —
Dutch and English and so on. When I'd studied the
Acts of the Apostles in school in England, our teacher,
the very erudite Mr. Roberts (cruelly nicknamed
"B.O. Roberts" by my schoolmates) had informed us
that glossolalia was a feature of many "mystery
cults". This was really interesting. But I was
convinced I could to it more convincingly than any of
them.

A few days later, I got my chance.

Dean was involved in a programme for troubled
teenagers called *Teen Challenge*. As I was both
troubled and a teenager, though perhaps not in the
usual heroin-in-the-alley running-around-in-gangs
variety, he took me along one day.

Once there, I was subjected to the kind of hard-
sell that now I realize is common to all these
operations, from scientology to Hare Krishna. I was
told how bad I felt about myself and how accepting
Jesus into my heart would take away the pain. People
were wildly praying and murmuring and there was
this blond guy shaking me over and over, shouting
"Say it! Say you accept Jesus as your Savior!"

Well, the mass hypnosis of the chanting and
praying and hullaballooing certainly was persuasive.
I was on the verge of saying yes, but my superpowers
saved me. I burst into a dramatic paean of
glossalalia, carrying on with gutturals and creaky
tones and peculiar glottal stops and all these things I
knew about from my lifelong fascination with
linguistics. It was the performance of a lifetime, and
from then on they all accepted me as having been
"born again," though I had actually managed to avoid

saying "yes."

Later, it would only take a week at Cambridge surrounded by my intellectual peers to make me "die again".

For now, though, my superpowers proved useful indeed. The next day, I attended a sort of prayer-meeting at the Middendorf home and I told Isabelle, "I spoke in tongues last night."

She cried out in glee and embraced me, and suddenly we were on track once more to do the *Rock Mass* in the ambassadorial residence.

***

The event was beautiful. First, it was summer and I was teaching at a summer music camp for American kids run by the multitalented Rita Liebermann, and we brought dozens of kids to the event. My friends, old and new, played — a lovely flute solo by flautist/ bassoonist Hugh Thirlway and and earnest oboe solo by his wife Christine; me on piano, and a rather touching performance of the *Gloria* by my sister Kiki.

Cookies and milk and a feel-good sermon by the Rev. Lewis, and the cameras of EO catching everything.

There was a dark side to this, though.

Months later, when Evangelische Omroep's documentary came out, they did in fact show a beautiful snippet from the *Mass* in which Kiki sang very charmingly. It was not a polished performance, the producer had told me, but there was something very magical, very special about it, and it certainly seemed so.

Bill spoke in interviews throughout the show

about his special relationship with Jesus, and yet ... I had a feeling that he and I shared a certain detachment.

I remembered that one time, when Isabelle was saying that her husband was spending too much time on music, he said to her, "All right, all right, I'll write a Jesus Symphony next," in a placating tone.

He never did.

But the dark side was more personal for me.

You see, the EO show had been edited in such a way that, segueing from one of Bill Middendorf's discussions of music, the *Gloria* from my *Rock Mass* appeared very much to be one of *his* compositions.

There were some little lower-third titles in corner, giving my name and my sister's name as the singer ... but there anyone watching the show would have assumed that not only had Bill Middendorf written his own music, but he had written *mine* as well.

Was I being punished for the insincerity of my conversion?

It would seem that a bargain with Jesus could have certain Faustian overtones....

***

Rather than risk offending the Almighty again, I decided that I should fix the problem in an upright, Anglican way. You see, when I handed in the form for the choral scholarship, I had written "C. of E." in the religion slot.

I had never, however, "had it done." I resolved to do so as quickly as possible.

Luckily, one of my best friends in London was the Reverend Douglas Bean, a minor canon at St. Paul's

Cathedral, whose wife was a singer and actress. He himself had written a bunch of religious pop songs, and I'd been in a band with him for a while, singing them in churches, one time even in Wormwood Scrubs prison, where Sir Michael Tippett had been jailed for pacifism.

He offered to do the deed for me in the basement of St. Paul's Cathedral. It was quickly done, and with great pomposity Douglas read out the rather pretentious list of Christian Names I had now given myself: Symon Iain Somtow Richert Venanzius. I never used any of those names again. Except for my real name, that is.

My godparents included Douglas's wife Mary and Angela Cunninghame, wife of the New Zealand Ambassador to the Netherlands.

As much as the first conversion had been emotional and drama-filled, the second was quiet and very English, and I got a certificate afterwards, which has been lost. Not everyone (let alone every Buddhist) can say he was baptized in St. Paul's Cathedral.

Religious conversion to get ahead in music was good enough for Gustav Mahler, and it was good enough for me.

A year later, my *Rock Mass* was performed in the chapel of St. Catharine's College, Cambridge, and this time, everyone who was there knew I'd written it.

Bill Middendorf, Frances Middendorf, and Somtow looking over a score during a recording session

Chapter Seven
A Crusader in Cambridge

In the brief time I had left before going to Cambridge, I learned that J. William Middendorf, II was being recalled to the United States. He was to take up the post of Undersecretary of the Navy.

Although I lived on Boston at the age of two for a short time, I really knew America only from television. But before he left, Bill assured me that this was not over. "You're coming to the States," he said, "and there will more symphonies. And marches! Marches! The Navy Band is the best in the world!"

There was a parting gift. It was only on loan, because Bill couldn't take it with him right away, but it was an amazing thing to have in our house on Laan Copes van Cattenburch — it was a genuine 18th

Century Kirkman harpsichord.   Never had I played anything so beautiful.

Cambridge was a revelation as I threw myself into music despite doing my degree in English.   Once a week, I met my Director of Studies, John Andrew, and handed him an essay. What I did was to set my alarm, scour the recesses of my memory at 5 am for an essay I had written at Eton for Michael Meredith, in my humble opinion the greatest teacher of all time. and then regurgitate that essay, typing it up on the portable Hermes typewriter which my father had purchased from his college room mate, Rupert Murdoch, for £5.   I would then deliver the essay to John's chambers, and by 4 pm I would be ready to appear in person for the tutorial and receive my A+.

You see, Michael Meredith had been such a brilliant teacher, and he had been my tutor (which is a Eton position rather like a sort of supervisor of studies, mentor, teacher all in one) for three years. He taught me how to think so well that I could turn thinking on and off like a light switch. Therefore, for at least a year or two at Cambridge, I didn't really have to do any work at all on my chosen subject.

I could concentrate entirely on music.

Only after a year or so did my director of studies start to catch on to the fact that I wasn't actually doing any work. He finally said to me, "Somtow, you have the prose style of an angel, but —" and he sighed — "you have nothing to say."

Too late.   I had become ensconced in the music community. My "unofficial" teachers, from whom I learned everything, included some of the greatest musicians and savants on offer. The legendary David

Willcocks was a towering presence (he had overseen the scariest exam I ever took in my life, the choral scholarship ear test — "Listen to this chord cluster!" Crash! "Sing the fourth note up from the bottom, please.") People like Roger Norrington were popping in to reinvent the classical style. I sang in one of the very first performances of the Monteverdi *Vespers* which had just been resurrected from the ash-heap, under Edward Higginbottom. Ian Kemp taught me everything I know about opera.

Other great intellects were also around and one could pop in on their lectures. Fred Hoyle was propounding the steady state theory and Stephen Hawking could still talk. Black holes were in the air. George Steiner showed up in our common room and propounded his theory of the Levels of Difficulty in art.

But my greatest teachers were my contemporaries because for the first time in my life I was hanging out with people my own age who had achieved far more than I had. Robert Saxton, in the next room, had actually been corresponding with Benjamin Britten since the age of 12 (yeah, we all made jokes about that) had been a student of Elizabeth Lutyens, and one of his pieces, the enthusiastically anal-retentive *Ritornelli and Intermezzi,* was about to be published by Chesters. Other brilliant composers included James Ellis at Kings and James Wood at Sussex College, a student of Nadia Boulanger ... these great composers were in my year and they were far, far farther ahead in their professional lives than I was. Instrumentalists, too: Robin Ireland, who became the violist for the well known quartet the Lindsays, Judith

Weir whom I knew as brilliant oboist, little knowing that she would later become one of England's leading composers and 'Master of the Queen's Music', amazing harp player Frances Kelly — one could go on and on.

They weren't however, at the time, composing operas, which is all that I really wanted to do ... it was the one art form that could finally bring together my two great loves, words and music.

I tried writing one at the age of 10, but it didn't progress much.

Maybe it was biting off a bit more than I could chew to try to do an opera of Goethe's *Faust*. I only managed a couple of pages of full score, and the vocal part had a range only half an octave.

The second opera, one I actually completed at Eton, at least in short score, was based on Ibsen's *Brand,* and its libretto was based on the original Dano-Norwegian text. Michael Meredith had arranged to send a copy to Den Norske Opera, and I'd received a politely condescending brushoff letter on Kirsten Flagstad's official stationery (though the great soprano was already dead.) That score is lost, though I keep hoping it will turn up in their archives.

My third attempt had been started when the Middendorfs were in Holland; it was to be a massive epic of the life of Michelangelo — and yes, this piece had its moments. I worked on it constantly during my first year, hoping to somehow manage a production.

In the midst of all this perfervid creativity, I got a call from the Hague. Philips had produced an LP of the *Holland Symphony.* My music (if you could call it mine) was on vinyl! (We didn't call it vinyl in those days.)

I couldn't wait to put it on the turntable.

***

As I listened, at first it was amazing.   But I gradually noticed that the recording didn't match what I had written. The conducting was boring — it sounded like someone halfheartedly going through the motions for a buck. But that wasn't what bugged me.

The notes themselves were different!

Okay, so some of the inelegances of my first scoring effort had been fixed.   The score was definitely easier on the ear in terms of some blemishes being glossed over.

But ....

Almost every melody had been altered. In pretty much every case, the melody had been moved away from something that had its basis in the Middendorf five-finger exercise or the Middendorf humming. The tunes had been altered in the direction of "normalcy". The harmonies had been "standardized."

Though the *Holland Symphony* was by no means a masterpiece, it did have a few shreds of originality. Bill's melodic ideas were not as hackneyed as the ones presented in this recording, and some of the harmonies that had been "fixed" were actually my childish attempts at original thought, or subtle ironic references.

As I sat there, I got more and more irate. As soon as it finished playing, I whipped off a red-hot letter demanding that my name be taken off the recording.

However, it was apparently too late for all that.

I comforted myself by throwing myself into my "real" music, which, under the influence of my friends and my environment, was maturing.

However, I soon received a phone call from Washington, DC. Phone calls were different in those days. One was ceremoniously summoned to the porter's lodge at the front gate of St. Catharine's, and the international phone call had to pass through a number of operators, with the discussion preceded by a few obligatory *"Can you hear me?"*s.

The call was to invite me to the United States as soon as possible (luckily, Cambridge took very long vacation breaks) Bill asked me about Cambridge and I told him about all the wonderful musicians. I told him that the early music revolution had its epicenter in Cambridge and it was the one place where one could find, for instance, a proficient player of the rebec.

"Think they could record *The Crusades?*"

And thus began the transatlantic segment of this collaboration. For Bill Middendorf had on his arrival been invited to chair the Wolf Trap Festival, created by a millionairess named Kay Shouse, and he wanted to present her with a sufficiently imposing gift. The Fourth Symphony was re-christened the *Wolf Trap Symphony* and this double album would be an amazing sequel to the *Holland Symphony* LP. This time, however, Bill didn't want a major label involved. He knew it would be better to keep control, so he decided to pay for the entire thing himself.

This is when my dearly beloved friend Robin

Ireland stepped into the Middendorf biosphere, followed shortly by a recording producer named Steve Paul who played the flute — he was older than us, was doing a doctorate of some kind, and had already produced many well known albums for Columbia Records.

Among Steve Paul's credits in that period, one stands out for me in particular: he had done an introduction and notes for *The Scatalogical Songs and Canons of W.A. Mozart.* Clearly my kind of guy.

Then there was Spaceward Sound Systems, the company that did the recording. This consisted of two long-haired guys, Mike Kemp and Gary Lucas. I grew to love them both very much, especially Gary, and was shocked to learn while googling him in preparation to writing this chapter that he had died a few months ago — I just missed be able to commuincate with him.

We were all so young then — and this is how I see them all in my mind's eye — so I was jolted by this death. Another reason, perhaps, to hurry up and tell this story, before I croak myself.

Robin offered to "fix" the orchestra and when they heard they would get a whopping $40 for each session, musicians signed up in droves.

This was not an orchestra that turned down their noses at the ambassador's amateurism or ridiculed my inexperience. He was not by then an ambassador or even Undersecretary of the Navy; he had been elevated to Secretary of the Navy, one of the most powerful positions in the American government. The Department of the Navy in the U.S. also encompasses the elite Marine Corps.

The Cambridge Symphony Orchestra, as it came

l. to r. Mike Kemp and Gary Lucas, ca. 1972

to be christened, were all my age, and were also just about the most sophisticated musicians you could find anywhere. You don't get to read music at Cambridge just by being a great performer — you have to have other qualities. Indeed, half the people in the orchestra weren't specifically doing music at Cambridge at all.

These were people who were ready to enjoy the delicious irony of the Middendorf aesthetic. They got the jokes, but they also got the earnestness, the underlying innocence of Bill Middendorf's vision.

The first day of recording was amazing, a real barrel of laughs. We had started with the scherzo from the *Wolf Trap Symphony*. It's sort of an Irish jig kind of melody but its final cadence has a strangely intellectual-sounding quadruplet laid over the triple meter.

After sight-reading the movement, everyone was in a very jolly mood. The symphony was a hit among these super-snooty intellectual kids, though perhaps not entirely for the reasons Bill Middendorf had in mind.

Even so, as Judith Weir said to me later, "That jig-thing — it's really got a kind of *charm.*"

After a day's hard work, the *Wolf Trap Symphony* was done. We met a few days later for *The Crusades*. This was only Bill's second symphony, and (since my orchestration experience had been growing exponentially between Middendorf symphonies) it had a few more technical faux pas than the Fourth — missing accidentals, left-out-doublings, and so on. But because the orchestra wasn't hostile or skeptical, I felt safe enough to rewrite bits on the fly.

Most thrilling of all was the presence of a small contingent of rebecs, nakers, recorders, and a lute.

When they played the first notes quoted from King Richard's melody, we all felt the frisson of a temporal intersection.

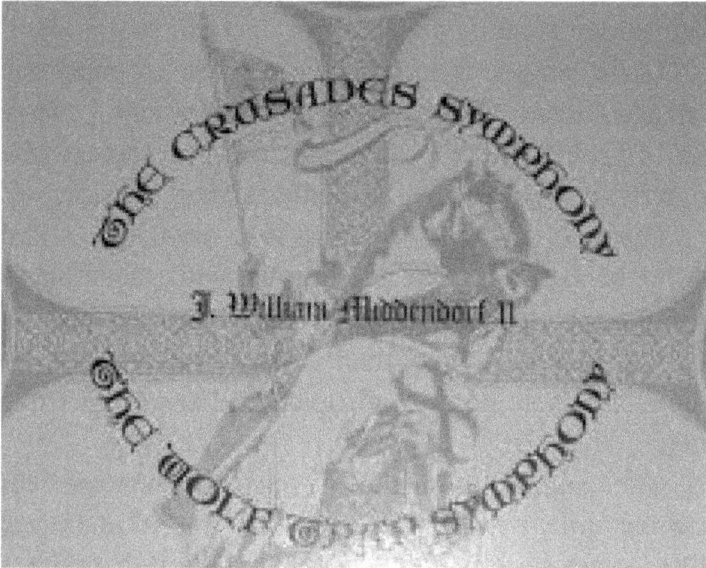

LP Cover of the Crusades Symphony

Yes, the battle scene was built of blocks of material awkwardly joined together and yes, the music had more of a whiff of Burbank than a fragrance of Palestine, but it had *something*.

What that *something* was, in my opinion, was not any technical expertise or skill on my part, nor the subtle irony that was omnipresent in these scores; that *something*, I believe, came from the man himself: though he was a man skilled in politics and diplomacy, both arts that require a constant awareness and deployment of the "dark side of the force." and though he was a shrewd businessman who had parlayed a fortune into a bigger fortune, another "dark side" sort of activity, in his artistic endeavors he saw the world with an enviable purity. He was the platonic essence of the human longing to create beauty and meaning.

I think that the story that Mike Kemp tells on the Spaceward website illustrates it best:

> To do the recording we assembled a "Cambridge Symphony Orchestra" of impressive size in the old Music School theatre in Downing Street, Cambridge. Somtow conducted and directed. The recording went well, and after it was all over we had to phone the US Pentagon to tell Mr JWM about it.
>
> Naturally we reversed the charge as in those days transatlantic calls were beyond the budget of a fledgling recording studio. After dialing the Pentagon and nervously asking to speak to the Secretary for the Navy, we were put through rapidly. We were surprised when he asked us to play the symphony to him over the phone, but of course we did.
>
> When it was over (some 25 minutes later) there was a breathless silence over the line, then he said "That was great, play it again". So we did.

Asking to hear the entire symphony over the phone from across the Atlantic Ocean — today that would be kind of like asking to hear it from the Moon — that was pure Bill Middendorf. And immediately saying "Play it again!" That, too, was pure Middendorf.

Even though I wasn't there, I can already see that childlike glint in the eye. (His daughter Frances has that same expression.) When he had that expression, he was, in the truest sense of the word, *beautiful.*

Seeing him in that state of bliss, longing myself to achieve such bliss but knowing I never could: in the end, it was this quality of his that kept me doing this for almost fifteen years.

The recording was mixed and mastered and pressed by EMI, so I had the opportunity to work at the legendary Abbey Road studios.

We spent almost as much time photographing ourselves crossing the street in imitation of the celebrated shot of the Beatles at Abbey Road, but unfortunately, all those photographs are lost.

Mike Kemp had this to say about pressing the disks:

> Anyway we finally pressed 1,000 vinyl disks of the performance for him, and later we were again impressed when he when he sent the US navy to the door of 19 VIctoria Street to collect the disks.
>
> This was in the form of a cavalcade of military limos, with a high ranking officer emerging and hammering on the door, followed by him and his underlings trying to fit into our tiny office.
>
> Together they sat at the desk and counted each of the disks. There were a few more than 1,000 pressed and they of course refused to take these. I think they regarded us rather suspiciously over the excess number, maybe supecting a subtle plot. Orders were after all to collect 1,000 disks, and I guess you don't mess with orders from the secretary to the US navy!
>
> Anyway, they finally departed happily with the disks and that's the last we heard.

J William Middendorf had become famous in Cambridge.   Pretty much everyone in the music department had been the beneficiary of one or more of the forty-dollar sessions fees.   More recordings were to come, and more ambitious ones — I imagine that the young musicians were quite well supplied with beer for quite a time through his largesse.

I also believe that of all the times that his music was performed in different countries, the performances at Cambridge went down better than anywhere else.   These were sophisticated musicians who appreciated the ironies and little bits of humour, but also saw in the music the composer's genuine drive, his passion to create real art.

***

But what of my own music? All this time, indeed, I was trying to get my opera *Michelangelo* produced. James Ellis had agreed to conduct.   Robert Saxton took one chorus rehearsal, and the chorus had managed to get one of the scenes right precisely once. I had talked Jacek Strauch (now a famous baritone, but then just another student at Cambridge) about the title role. My aunt in Thailand paid a lot of money to have a printer make bound copies of the score.

Unfortunately, I ran out of money, and my score languished. It has still never been performed.

That might be a blessing: I'm a lot more practical a composer now than I was then, and there *were* things in this opera that were just "showing off". I do wish, sometimes, it could have been produced.   It seemed to me that, as long a piece bore the name *Middendorf* and was composed in the style of a slightly dull nineteenth-century composer, I could always get the money, but if something bore my own name, it could not.

The seed for a schizoid crisis had been planted; though I did not know it, an eruption was only a matter of time.

An eruption of a different kind, however, was about to occur. A Christmas break was looming, and I had been invited to the United States for a new orgy of humming and symphonizing. I did not know that this invitation had been accompanied by a maëlstrom of familial upheaval.

I was about to get crushed between the Scylla of Bill's passion and the Charybdis of Isabelle's fury.

Chapter Eight
An Exorcism in the Suburbs

I was now about to see the Middendorfs in all their native splendor — no ambassadorial mansions, no police escorts, no royal tea-times. It was the Christmas season and Nixon was having troubles, mired in scandal, about to go down.

McLean, Virginia was a suburb for the well-heeled. I've recently read on Wikipedia that it is the third wealthiest city in America. It's located very close to the CIA, and very accessible to the Pentagon, where J. William Middendorf now held sway.

I arrived at the Middendorf household like a visiting sultan. I would leave ignominiously, after a botched exorcism.

All seemed well at first. Bill fetched me from the airport himself. The family greeted me with apparent pleasure, though I later realized that in some cases it was feigned.

America was a virgin territory to me, despite having lived there as a two-year-old. Everything was alien and beautiful, especially the snow, the impressive highway, the winding path into McLean, the house which, very weirdly to my Eurocentric mind, had only one level but sprawled a lot, and had a lot of grounds.

The house itself was very far from the baroque splendor I had imagined for the Middendorfs; I remember that it was quite angular, and strangely modern, like a concatenation of shoeboxes. I was ushered into a room which was, I think, actually John's room (my apologies, forty years later, for that!) and soon I was in the living room, and talking about marches.

Marches ... and opera.

You see, those mediaeval instruments, that melody written by Richard the Lionhearted, those sonorities hadn't left his mind since the folks at Spaceward played the tape over the phone to him twice through.

As I sat in his living room, playing Verdi-like riffs on the piano, he was musing about Richard's love life. "Yeah, I realize he was kind of a pansy," he said, "but what if he met a real woman, one no one in their right mind could refuse?"

"I daresay Richard could have fallen for an exotic dusky beauty," I said, getting into the mood. I was thinking, He probably needs another big Hollywood-type score. *The Crusades* had been quite a short symphony at 20-odd minutes. Perhaps he was thinking of an expanded version with a Miklos Rozsa-type love theme thrown in.

"Pahlavi," he said. "Can we call her Pahlavi?"

"Isn't that the Persian royal family's surname?" I asked him.

"Well, sure," he said, "but the audience will never know."

He rather liked the name Pahlavi for a heroine (I suspect he had Sophia Loren, who played Ximene in *El Cid,* in his mind's eye.)

On the other hand, perhaps *Roxane* would sound more feminine....

Apparently he had run into the name recently — or someone by that name. Since it was the name of one of Alexander the Great's wives, it had a historic ring. Alexander's Roxane was a princess of Sogdiana which was in the furthermost edge of the Persian Empire, so it still fell within the Persian sphere ... and for some reason Bill thought it would be a great name for Richard's lover ... "She could be Saladin's daughter!" he said, imagining some kind of forbidden love scenario. "Nah, let's make her a niece, in case Saladin's daughter was a real person."

"Okay."

"I want to spell her name in an exotic way. I think the Persians spelled it something like ... R-o-k-h-s-a-n-n-e-h." Not being an expert on Old Persian, I took him at his word.

"Now, play me some dramatic music. Richard is imprisoned and his troubadour Blondel hears his voice floating down from a tower...."

I did sort of a soundtrack to an imaginary silent film — the way theater pianists must have done in the good old days. "No, no," he said, "more dramatic, kind of like this — ba BUM ba bum, ba BUM ba bum."

I finally played something he liked and he said, "Now can you help me think of the words?"

It was only then that I, who had composed three abortive, unperformed operas, understood that I was about to embark on someone else's....
***

I offered to make Thai food for the family lunch the next day. Also, Isabelle took some of the kids and me on a tour of the Washington Monument and Lincoln Memorial. I felt as though I were in an idyllic sort of sitcom ... I was the visiting oriental being shown the joys of American civilization.

I thought I was having a great time, but in the middle of the tour, Mrs. Middendorf glared at Johnny. He, had, apparently, misbehaved, though I can't say that I noticed. "I'll deal with you when we get back," she told him. He nodded somberly.

On arriving back at the house, she and Johnny retired to an inner room and, from what I could overhear, he appeared to be receiving a sound thrashing. He emerged, clenching back his tears. This household was a little less like the Brady Bunch than I had thought.

Later, I would wonder whether Isabelle wasn't actually taking out on her child the anger she felt against me. That made me feel very guilty. Perhaps one day I'll be able to tell him I'm sorry I caused him pain.

I decided on a "See no evil, hear no evil" approach and that evening spent some time working on a libretto for an opera about Richard and Rokhsanneh.   I typed up the following on a conveniently located Selectric II (God, how I loved that masterpiece of 1970s high-tech!) — tapping away in a fever of excitement. which must have kept the household up all night.

PROLOGUE

The curtain rises on a desolate European landscape.   In the background, we see the ramparts of a castle from which a lonely tower arises. As the prelude music begins to play, BLONDEL, *a ministrel, enters. His clothes are in tatters; he has obviously been traveling a great distance.*

BLONDEL
O sorrow! Dark despair!
The quest for my vanished master
Is all in vain!
King Richard! My lost master!
Where have they imprisoned you?
Your armies have returned
To heal their battle wounds
On England's soil, fair England's soil;
You alone have not returned.
For many years
I have been wand'ring through Europe;
I, your troubadour Blondel!
Before each castle wall I sing
The melody which you have written,
Hoping to hear an answer —
My quest is vain!
Castle after castle have I tried.

And no reply has come forth
From those dungeon walls!

Blondel sees the castle in the background. He moves closer to the castle. There is no way to scale the walls.

BLONDEL

Forbidding and impregnable
Here stands a mighty fortress!
Before I end my fruitless search
I will sing my song once more.

Accompanying himself on the lute, Blondel sings.

BLONDEL

"Joy and delight do I banish from my heart,
Singing of sorrow with troubadour's art.
How shall I rest when the city of God
Groans under pain of the Saracen rod?
O Jerusalem! O my city!
Shall I be happy when thou art in chains?
Many tears of love and pity
Shall requite thy captive pains."

Suddenly, from the tower, we hear the voice of KING RICHARD COEUR DE LION. *Blondel looks up at the tower in amazement.*

RICHARD

"How shall I rest, thou city of Gold?
Noble my knights; my barons are bold!
Joy and delight do I banish from me
Till I have freed thee from captivity."

BLONDEL

Praise be to God!
It is my master surely.
None but we two did know this melody.
King Richard — it is I!

RICHARD

My faithful troubadour!

Richard appears at the prison window, haggard and unkempt.

RICHARD

Return to my court in fair England,
And tell them I am shamefully misused.
I am a King — yet must endure
The terrible torment of imprisonment.
I am imprisoned by an evil traitor.
Kept from my homeland and my people.
Make haste to see that I am ransomed
And returned once more to fair England.

BLONDEL

Now all my years of searching
Have borne fruit!
I will bring rescue
With might of arms —
Humble the baron
Who presumes to cage my Lord!

RICHARD

Do not use arms,
My faithful Blondel.
For in this war against the heathen,
I have learned that wars bring grief.
Daily I pray God will forgive me
That I presumed to know his will.
Listen, my faithful troubadour,
I will unfold to you
A bitter tragedy,
So great that it will bring unbidden
The tears to your eyes.
So I will recount the battles
And the loves of my crusade —
Which now shall live
Before your eyes!

The curtain falls, and we segue without a break to the Overture.

To be sure, this was at best a mediocre exemplar of the librettist's art. It owed a lot to such appalling wordsmiths as Salvadore Cammarone, whose libretto for Verdi's *Il Trovatore* has the most confusing plot of all time, and perhaps even a little to W.S. Gilbert in his "taking the mickey out of Italian opera" mode.

Here and there were clear echoes of operas I was really into at the time. For example, I see now that the phrase "shamefully misused" was borrowed from Tippett's opera *King Priam*. In that opera, it refers to Hector's treatment of Achilles' corpse.

However, when larded with sufficient orchestral bombast, the result would be pretty effective. I was sure of it.

I barely slept because the prospect of working on an opera that might actually be performed was much more exciting than whether I would have my name on it.

***

In the morning, I woke up to the sound of a woman screaming. *"Somtow! Get out of this house!"* It was terrifying. The screaming continued, at times incoherent. Then, to amazement, I heard *"Somtow! You - you - you - shithead!"* a word I never dreamed could come from the pious lips of — Mrs. Middendorf!

Quickly I put on some clothes and went into the living room. Isabelle Middendorf was in a wild rage and Bill was trying to calm her down. When she saw me, she rushed over and started pummeling me with her fists. I tried to fend off the bows, which were more bizarre than painful, and wasn't quite sure if this was some kind of initiation ritual. "You and your music! You've ruined our lives."

As you can imagine, I was taken aback. "I'm only writing music," I said. "I'm not trying to destroy your family. Bill *loves* you."

"No! Billy loves *you!* He doesn't care about us anymore! He lavishes trips and gifts on you! Shithead! *Shithead!*"

Although *The Exorcist* was a few years in the future, I thought I could bring her to her senses by pushing her Pentecostal buttons. "You're - possessed!" I said. (Surely the sudden attack of Tourette's was proof of that.)

Bad idea. "*You're* possessed!" she shrieked. And then she began waving her arms over me and shouting in a tone of sacerdotal command, "Get *out* of him in the name of Jesus! I cast you out!"

I didn't quite know what to do next, so I lifted up two fingers and started making the sign of the cross over her, and saying, "No, no, get out of *her* in the name of Jesus!"

So we stood there, exorcising each other, for several minutes. Until Bill Middendorf decided he'd had enough and dragged her off into the bedroom.

Exhausted, I sank back into a chair.

I heard some carrying on from the inner room, but after a while it fell silent. Good, I thought, they must have made up.

At that moment, the phone rang.

I don't know why I picked it up — but someone in

another room picked it up too so I was just about to put it down when I heard a voice — a gravelly yet tremulous voice that I *knew.*

"Bill ... I'm going through *hell,* here."

I put the phone down like the proverbial hot potato.

I *knew* that voice from countless TV broadcasts. It *had* to be. Who could ever forget *I am not a crook?*

Stunned at having been exorcised and then hearing the voice of Richard M. Nixon, I just sat there, wondering what would befall next.

What could I do? I couldn't very well leave the house. In those days, I didn't even know how to drive, let alone on the wrong side of the street.

Presently, we were all summoned to lunch.

No one said a word. Everyone just stared at their food. No one ate much.

At length, Isabelle Middendorf spoke up. "You may have noticed that I'm wearing a lot of makeup, Somtow," she said.

To be honest, I had not. The morning had been so fraught with drama that I hadn't really studied her face.

She cleared her throat to make sure that she had everyone's full attention. "I've put on all this makeup," she said, "to cover up the fact that my husband gave me a black eye defending you."

Too shocked to respond, I finished my lunch. No one said another word.

I got up and packed my belongings. It was Christmas.

***

Remaining in McLean was out of the question and Bill Middendorf decided that I was to stay at the Army and Navy Club in Farragut Square.

"You do have a tie, don't you?" he asked, before I got into his car. "If not, they'll lend you one at the front desk."

Now this club was a tremendous spectacle. For one thing, it was a "no girls allowed" place — women were allowed only in the lobby and in the top floor dining room, which they had to reach by elevator, to avoid being seen in any of the halls. It was a glorious expansion of the boys' treehouse concept. Oh, there were a few women, I believe, but they were the help. There may have been women, but there were certainly no *ladies.*

After waiting for me to settle into my room, Bill met me in some kind of large unused room that had an upright piano.

"Let's work on some marches," he said, I *really* want to write some marches. I've got a great melody in my mind."

***

Chapter Nine
A Circumstance
without Pomp

This was the march that he hummed to me, on a cold winter's night, with my demons safely cast out and a solid meal sticking to my ribs....

"Sounds a bit familiar," I said, "though I can't quite place it — *Oh!*"

For what J. William Middendorf had hummed to me was of course a slightly transmuted version of the thing that is heard at every graduation ceremony in

America ... the *Pomp and Circumstance No. 2* by Edward Elgar.

So, on the piano, I played the opening phrase of the Elgar. "Yup!" he said happily. "You see, I only had to change one note."

I believe this march eventually became the *Library of Congress March*. It was premiered before all sorts of dignitaries a couple of years later.

***

We had several more evenings of marches, and the opera, whose plot was becoming ever more baroque.

Bill wanted to have all the elements of grand opera, including a dance sequence, so the plot was something like this:

> Rokhsanneh, glamorous and sexy niece of Saladin, is ordered to perform the Dance of Death, a kind of Dance of the Seven Veils at the end of which she stabs a Christian prisoner. Dying, the prisoner forgives her. Curious about this, she says, "What is this? Forgive the one who killed you?"
>
> The prisoner then preaches a mini-sermon about Christian forgiveness, so inspiring her that she bursts into a huge aria and, upon successful completion of a belting top D flat, flees the comfort of her Uncle's palace to find King Richard.
>
> He converts her to Christianity, but alas, she converts him to sex, and as he is no longer chaste, it becomes harder for him to be a true soldier of God.
>
> A climactic battle occurs which Rokhsanneh watches from a towering precipice. (I don't know if Jerusalem had any such conveniently located precipices, but hey, it's an opera.) To her horror, Richard's horse stumbles and throws him and — singing another rousing aria — she puts on his spare

armour which happens to be lying around and rides off
into battle herself.

Mistaken for her paramour by her Uncle, she is
dispatched by him.   Saladin cries out "What have I
done" as the soaring "Praise to Allah" leitmotif bursts
out in the orchestra.   Richard arrives just in time to
sing a final duet as she dies in his arms, Jerusalem
burning in the distance.

The Crusaders pick up their weapons and sadly,
tragically prepare for the long march home, chanting
Pange lingua as they schlep off into the west.

Whew! Unmitigated spectacle!

I want to say this: I was resentful that I'd failed to
get my own operas off the ground.   Now I was
writing one which, I was sure, *would* in fact produced.
So I threw myself into it. I had learned a lot about
orchestration since my bumbling misfires in the
Holland Symphony. I decided that this would be lush
and Wagnerian.   Triple woodwind, the trademark
mediaeval instruments, stratospheric divas, chorus,
dance, the kitchen sink. After all, there was someone
who, at a pinch, could just pay for the whole thing,
even if it meant auctioning off the odd Rembrandt.

And now, as a reward for working so hard, and
perhaps in compensation for having had to endure an
ignominious exorcism, I was being sent to "the most
exciting city in the world" — as Bill liked to call it —
New York. I was going to get to see opera at the Met.
***

Before I left, though, Frances Middendorf came
to the Army and Navy Club to join me for dinner.
She met me in the lobby and then we took the secret
elevator to the dining room.

There was one detail I've never forgotten. When they brought her the menu, it had no prices on it.

It was the ladies' menu, and ladies should never have to bother their little heads about what things cost. Oh, what a different world it was then!

It was nice to hang out with someone my own age. And she was smart, and perceptive, and above all she had a great sense of humor and she well understood the comic subtext of what her father and I were cooking up. At that dinner, we tried to laugh at the foibles of her parents, but then she said some very serious things to me. "You've gotta understand, Somtow," she said, "My parents' relationship has always been unusual. It's because long before they were married, they were brought up as brother and sister because of their parents' remarriage."

"You mean, even though they are not blood relatives, it's a kind of incest?"

"I mean sometimes there's a sibling dynamic. It's the way they fight. Like siblings."

I had noticed that she called him *Billy,* an odd way to address a grown man unless you've known him since childhood. I wondered whether their union might have something to do with money — keeping it all in the family or something. In Asia, such a marriage would be the norm, not the exception.

It would have been rude to ask, however. So I didn't.

***

I got to stay in the Union Club in New York, which was the Army and Navy Club Squared. No woman allowed there, either, and the help pretty much grovelling: "You have a telephone call, sir, at your leisure, I'll have a phone brought to your sofa, sir, at your leisure...." The level of staff subservience was almost comparable to typical upper class homes in Bangkok. Interesting to see that in an egalitarian society like America there was still a segment of the populace that enjoyed being kowtowed to like oriental potentates.

As time went by, I went to New York more than once, always generously subsidized by Bill. It was always the Union Club or the Plaza.

Amazingly, I got to see the Chagall-designed production of *The Magic Flute,* which had Anna Moffo and Hermann Prey in it. I laughed and cried and was just overwhelmed. I saw an impressive *Otello,* but don't remember who was in it.

I got to walk around the museums, look at Egyptian temples and dinosaurs.

Purchased my first "work of art" you could call it — not a Rembrandt, but the Chagall lithograph *Magic Flute* poster which the Met was selling for an astonishing $75.

I lost the poster after only three days; I went up to visit a friend in Connecticut, and she offered to get it framed for me in time for my next visit — unfortunately it was apparently stolen when she moved house.

Since it's worth several thousand bucks now, I've been bummed out for some 45 years over this. I've got several copies of the second printing, but that isn't really worth a lot of money. It looks beautiful, though, and one of them hangs in the Opera Siam office. Another above my piano in my home.

It reminds me about so many things I've lost,
wandering from country to country.

***

Hermann Prey in the Chagall-designed Magic Flute

In between becoming a symphonic sausage
factory, I also had to do school work. As I explained,
in my second year they had started to notice that I
wasn't paying much attention to the subject I was
ostensibly studying — English.

But I was about to have to deliver a bit of original
thought in the form of a brief dissertation. In those

days, regurgitation wasn't allowed for these things. I had to think of an original subject, and I thought of my friend from Eton, the Hon. Guy Greville, whose father was the Earl of Warwick.

Guy was an unruly kid with dashing charisma. I recently reconnected with him after almost half a century. He had become the Earl himself by then, and was on about his third Countess. He hadn't changed one bit despite much debauchery in the House of Lords.

Guy's family tree included one of the most obscure poets of the 17th Century, Fulke Greville, Lord Brooke, and I picked this poet as the subject of the dissertation, figuring I wouldn't have much competition when I wrote about "the Symbology of Fulke Greville's poetry in the context of Seventeenth Century Perceptions of Art."

Unfortunately, the thing was due on my return from the United States, and I hadn't been able to find a copy of Fulke Greville's poetry in any American bookstore.

Amazingly, Bill Middendorf used his Library of Congress privileges and found me this rare tome, which looked as if it hadn't been opened in a hundred years.

Every second that I wasn't ghost-writing operas and marches or imbibing the heady cultural life of New York, I was holed up in the Plaza Hotel bashing out this dissertation.

But so absent-minded had I become that I actually arrived back in Cambridge without this document and I had no clue where I had left it.

Panicking, I asked for help from Bill Middendorf,

and someone in his office tracked the manuscript to the garbage chute of the Plaza Hotel.

It's clear that these luxury hotels actually earn their stars! I got the ms. back, just a little bit stained.

My first (and subsequent) visits to the United States were only a few weeks long, but each was intense. Each time, Bill Middendorf was generous to a fault. Top hotels or snooty clubs, opera tickets, and cheques.

Because of Bill, I got to see Grace Bumbry in *Salome.* I sat in the front row when John Pritchard was conducting *The Barber of Seville,* so close to the orchestra that when I murmured "Flat!" at a certain soprano note, he turned around to me and said, "Yes, you're right."

And my fees went up. For the full score of the opera, I was getting paid by the page. For most orchestral works I was averaging $100 a minute (of finished product). $400 per march may not seem much today, but on a good day I could write out three of them, though my fingers would get pretty sore.

The marches were the most economical for me, because I only composed them in short score. I never learned how to compose properly for band, but what with being Secretary of the Navy, Bill had access to a host of competent arrangers.

I was able to deliver the dissertation on time, and I finished "Part I" of the English degree (a two year programme) and was awarded a "II.1."

Under the Cambridge grading system of the time, one or two people in each subject would receive a first (or distinction). Virtually every one else would receive a second class, but there were two divisions of second, the II.1 (which was a small select grouping, though not quite as elite as the I) and the II.2, which would basically encompass pretty much the entire year. A III, also available, was ignominious.

Today, "firsts" are as common as "A"s are in the U.S. system, but in those days were rare. Considering that I had not gone to any lectures (except those not about my subject) and had spent all my spare time in the music faculty, I considered a II.1 pretty damn respectable.

At the end of my second year in Cambridge, I assumed that I would be finishing my degree in English, but destiny took me in another direction.

Chapter Ten
A Diva with a Dagger

It would take more than a few days of scratching to produce an entire opera. But in the summer of 1974 — momentous in American politics, to be sure — momentous things happened in my life as well.

My father was reassigned to Japan, and my parents invited, as is the custom, to a private farewell luncheon with Queen Juliana. But — as was *not* the custom — an invitation came for me as well.

Out came the police escort and the ambassadorial car, this time driven by our chauffeur, Eduardo. The same lightning-fast, fairy-tale scenery drive to Soestdijk Palace. This time, however, I was no longer a shrinking violet; I fully planned to engage in conversation.

Prince Bernhard was present as well. This was long before he got caught up in fiscal shenanigans. This meal was to be a little more formal than the tea-time, but I felt a little more prepared.

They were incredibly charming as they greeted my parents, and soon we were ushered into an impressive private dining room.

To my horror, the first course was a shrimp cocktail. I am highly allergic to vinegar which was present in the sauce, and I had been known to vomit copiously at the slightest whiff, let alone spoonful.

Nevertheless, the rules of protocol demanded that I take at least a bite of it, and I wasn't about to get my parents embroiled in a diplomatic incident. Bravely, I took a spoonful. My gorge rose. I wondered if there was somewhere I could duck away so I could safely throw up, but at that moment, His Royal Highness the Prince of the Netherlands decided to address me.

"So, Somtow," he said, "What is your opinion of Messiaen?"

Clearly, since I was a "modern composer", the Prince had been given a list of topics, of which Oliver Messiaen seemed to have topped the list. I don't think His Royal Highness was a aficionado of Messiaen per se. I was in no state to discourse intellectually about Messiaen — I was too busy trying to avoid vomiting on the Queen.

(Years later, when George Bush had a similar problem on a state visit to Japan, I remember feeling a twinge of sympathy, though by then I had been mostly purged of any Republican leanings.)

It took about twenty minutes for me to return to normal, and I must say that only my mother noticed that my countenance had been through all the colors of the rainbow in those twenty minutes. The rest of the lunch was a blur, but at the end, the Queen presented my father was an impressive Order — one of those "House of Orange" sorts of things. This made him some kind of knight.

"And," the Queen said, "because of your contribution to the *Holland Symphony,* I also have something for Mr. Sucharitkul the Younger." It was a signed photograph in a beautiful blue official frame.

My mother took the photo into custody, saying that I would only lose it, so now that I am 65, it is still on display at my parents' home.

Later, she told me she was really proud of me for not vomiting. "I know what you went through," she said. "You really took one for the team."

***

The next vacation, I flew to Japan instead of to the States. To my surprise, I was invited to appear as the representative of Thailand at an Asian Composer's Conference in Kyoto.

A Mr. Nabeshima came to our house, a mansion built in the form of a French chateau, in the upscale Meguro area — it had once belonged to the Kikkoman sauce-producing family. I submitted an excerpt from *Michelangelo,* my unproduced opera, but his soprano wife took one look at the top F and turned her thumbs down. So I sat down in the dining room of the residence, which had a really big flat surface for stacking music paper, and wrote a piece called *Cemeteries* in a white-heat.   It was scored for violin and piano.

Later, Robert Saxton would nickname my piece *Lavatories.* I told you he was anal-retentive.

I had been in Japan for only a matter of days when I find myself on a train to Kyoto.   Robin Ireland, my friend from Cambridge, joined me a few days later.

This conference was life-changing.

Cemeteries was performed by the Czech concertmaster of the Kyoto Municipal Symphony, a tall, balding, mustachioed, blondish man in a white dinner jacket.   He played it with a lugubrious profundity, pulling out all the stops and managing its preposterously difficult technique with aplomb. After the performance I went up on the stage and I found myself being squeezed in a huge bear-hug. "Maestro!" he said to me.

It was the first time I'd ever been called that.

At this conference, I got the first inkling that here was a world full of composers, with a shared camaraderie, a feeling of *us* against the world.   I was 21 years old.

Everyone there was at least ten years older than me.   Among them, the man who would become Japan's leading opera composer, Shigeaki Saegusa; older composers who were already legendary, like Takemitsu and Mayuzumi ... and composers from other countries like Taiwan's Hsu Tsang-Houei and the irrepressible José Maceda, who had composed *Udlot-Udlot,* a composition for 1,000 people hitting little sticks.

Despite my youth, these people were treating me as their peers. The reception of my piece by an audience of people who actually knew music was intoxicating. In the moment that the violinist called me *maestro,* I had an epiphany.

I was a real composer.

Not a composer of fake 19th century symphonies, but someone who was creating a new fusion of Asian music with European music of the twentieth century.

I had an identity.

Or did I?

Flushed with excitement, I fired off an letter to my director of studies at Cambridge. I told about my experience here and how it had changed my whole *Weltanschauung.* I couldn't very well go on with English. I *had* to switch to music.

Switching to music would mean doing Part II of the music tripos in a year, without the two year preparation of Part I, which I'd already completed in English Literature. That is, jumping to the hardest part without any of the preparatory work.

Cambridge was, at least in those days, a place that trusted its undergraduates — the lectures weren't compulsory, you saw your Director of Studies once a week and it was basically "So what are you doing this week, have a glass of sherry —" To get a degree, you had to basically complete *any* two parts which did not have to be the same subject.

Cambridge did not bother to write back, so I assumed they weren't going to let me switch. Oh well, I told myself, it's just a year, and then I'll dive into music.

When I arrived back, however, everyone seemed

to already know I had gone over to the music department. In fact, they acted as though I'd never been anywhere else.

Musically it was to be an exciting year to be a choral scholar. For one thing, the C.U.M.S. choir was doing big things, because the year was to be David Willcocks' swan song, so Mahler 8 and Beethoven's *Missa Solemnis* were on the docket. I'd also signed up to sing in a double bill of *Trial by Jury* and *The Pirates of Penzance*. Though I had halfway given up hope of getting someone to perform *Michelangelo,* I started a new opera called *Interfaces*.

Robert Saxton looked over the opening of the new opera and said, "Good heavens. The pitches are quite carefully worked out."

I think this was a compliment.

Amid all this, there came a message from the Pentagon. J. William Middendorf wanted to record part of the opera we were composing. He also wanted to hear his Violin Concerto, a piece we'd thrown together a few months earlier.

***

What can I say about the Middendorf Violin Concerto? Well, the first movement is strongly influenced by the Brahms concerto; the second by the Tchaikovsky; the third by the Beethoven. So I would say that it betrays the influence of three of the world's top ten violin concertos — some would say the top three.

The violinist we found to interpret this chimerical opus was Robin Stowell, subsequently of the

Academy of Ancient Music and the English Concert, so certainly an early music expert. He is now Professor of Music at Cardiff University. He was and is a fine musician. His only regret, he told me, is "we didn't have quite enough time ... there were so many little things I wanted to do with the concerto, but we didn't have quite enough time...."

I must include this quote from Yehudi Menuhin, an important figure from my school years because his son Jeremy was at Eton at the same time as me and he was an influential figure in the Windsor Festival which often used our school's facilities (I remember a fine *Dido and Aeneas* that used our newly built Farrer Theater, for example.) This is what Lord Menuhin had to say about the Middendorf violin concerto:

> I listened to the Violin Concerto and its spontaneous warmth and melodiousness are among its most pleasing qualities. Surely you must be the first Secretary of the Navy to have composed a violin concerto! How fortunate we are that so sensitive and responsible position in government is vested in a person of such great musical sensibility as yourself.

Well, yes. The concerto did have a lot of charm. It wasn't nearly as "amusing" as the earlier works ... to an unsuspecting listener, it was no chimaera at all. And lively melodies! No need to have someone come in a "correct" any contrapuntal felicities. I was really honing my craft.

***

Recording two scenes from the opera, now titled *The Lion and the Rose,* was almost ridiculously exciting. First, in the rôle of Rokhsanneh, we had managed to engage Mary Wells, wife of the new head of music at King's College, Phillip Ledger (who had taken over from David Willcocks.) Mary Wells was a star at Covent Garden who left opera to marry. Her voice was of Wagnerian size, colored by an unusual vibrato. It reminded me most of Inge Borkh, whom I had seen in *Die Frau ohne Schatten* at Covent Garden. It was cavernous yet with a hidden frailty. Having her do the role was simply magnificent. She had been coached in performing this rôle by no less a figure than Judith Weir.

Richard the Lionheart was sung by Bob Chilcott, today known to all choir singers around the world. He was a tenor and a choral scholar at King's — having previously been a boy soprano in their choir school and performed a famous, bestselling recording of the *Pie Jesu* from the Fauré *Requiem*.

The captive brutally slain in the Dance of Death was sung by Richard Suart, a bass who was later much in demand in comic and character roles. The two male singers were young choral scholars from King's; Mary Wells was a seasoned pro with the proverbial "voice that could shatter glass." Of course, via the miracle of the recording studio, the balance was perfect.

Somtow conducting; Steve Paul producing; modern and mediaeval instruments in the Cambridge Symphony Orchestra

Sitting in the audience was Phillip Ledger himself, with his eyes closed throughout as this Wagnerian/ Straussian orgy of sound welled up around him.

Another member person sitting in the audience was Paul Webster. He had come to St Catharine's a year later than Robert Saxton and I had, and he was an obscenely accomplished musician and pianist. He used to sightread his way through Strauss scores from beginning to end as entertainment. Paul was given a particularly important job. He had a full score on his lap and at the end of every take he would say, "The second trombone part, bar 17, should be a B flat not a B natural" and so on — for the parts had been copied by hand by an army of young scribes and my handwriting was not necessarily the clearest.

The session started well. Judith gleefully remarked, "Oh how brilliant, how do you manage to make it sound like Mahler and Strauss and all those guys all at once?"

I myself was swept away by the overblown drama of the music, conducting with great abandon, and slowing down for the juicy bits as though I were Furtwängler conducting *Tristan*. I certainly overdid it, for halfway through the first session Mary Wells said, "Somtow, we're not going to have any breath left if you're so self-indulgent!"

It was Paul Webster who took me aside and said, "Somtow, somehow this session is different. This opera is getting to you."

"What do you mean?"

"It's not as *fun* as it was last time. I mean, you're taking this really *seriously*. Like it's great art or something. You should relax."

It was an identity crisis. I had manifested two discrete selves — the serious artist trying to fuse alien cultures, and this ironic American composer of 19th century ditties. These incompatible mirror-entities were refusing to stay separate.

***

The album this time would be mastered and pressed a little closer to home for Bill Middendorf, with an outfit called "Sounds Reasonable, Inc." — SRI — coming on board. This would enable Bill, now known as "SecNav" in the government's complex system of acronyms, to be able to observe and engage in the process more fully.

Thus it was that I came into contact with Richard McCracken, Bill Middendorf's new assistant — or "fixer" — for dealing with music. Dick, as he was known, was a pretty straitlaced military sort of person — I believe he was a marine — and had an extensive and knowledgable background in military music — brass bands, symphonic bands, and course, marches. He was also an arranger, and from my first encounter with him I could see that he viewed me as an inconvenience — and that he thought things would go a lot smoother if I weren't around at all.

The problem is that while Dick knew everything about band music, his ignorance about classical music was pretty much total. Thus he had a tendency to try to talk Bill Middendorf out of things that were absolutely essential, and to want to reduce everything to four-bar phrases. He didn't approve of asymmetry at all. And he had an unshakeable belief in his own talents and infallibility.

While mixing the master at SRI, Dick insisted on many very bizarre things — such as making the levels as equal as possible and having loud and soft bits evened out. He told me (and the SecNav) that this was *always* done — which of course isn't true with classical music, which gives the engineer a chance to show off the dynamic range of the recording. He didn't listen when I told him that the slow movement of the Violin Concerto started piano and built up to forte. He made them flatten it all.

My handwriting is a little difficult at times, but he also appeared to almost purposefully misunderstand things or not to realize that some directions in classical music are not in English — reading tam-tam as tom-tom, insisting that "l.v." which stands for "laissez vibrer" was actually "let ring." and pooh-poohing my translation of my own handwriting.

He even managed to usurp my role as amanuensis once or twice, getting in between the SecNav's humming and my pianistic rendition in order to carry off the rich prize of one of the SecNav's melodies for himself.

The way that McCracken managed to insinuate himself into the Middendorf universe can be seen, I think, rather clearly in this, the back of the *Lion and the Rose* album, shown below.

What is the largest personal name on this album cover, larger than the composer's name, the "arranger's" name, the soloist's name? The only name blazoned as a personal signature, surrounded by a sea of white space, proclaiming "authorship" in as self-aggrandizing way as possible?

Yes. Richard A. McCracken, who was the author of — not the concerto — not the opera — not the libretto — not the singing — not the playing — but of the liner notes.

McCracken was one of the many people whose type I had seen circulating around Bill Middendorf from the Holland days. For Middendorf was exceedingly wealthy, yet, in some ways, an innocent — or at least he allowed himself to appear so when it suited him. There were a lot of people standing around sucking up and waiting for handouts, and I had McCracken pegged for one of the smarmier ones from the start.

When a person is this rich, such hangers-on are inevitable and a little paranoia-inducing. Even Isabelle's witch-doctor-like exorcism scene the previous Christmas had had as one of its motives the protection of her husband from a parasite.

I believe that Bill was perfectly aware of who was a parasite and who was not. But he had compassion. He often let people take advantage of him and think him an easy mark, when actually he saw right through them.

McCracken did have an exaggerated vision of his own abilities, however. He had written the liner notes himself, when he could easily have asked me to do so; after all, I actually knew something about the music being played.

Instead, these are the kinds of platitudes he came up with:

> The undertaking of composing an opera in our present era is almost a lost art. The dedication and research required for such an undertaking is sometimes too much for present day composers ... the entire opera is approximately two and one-quarter hours. The listener will find that the small taste of *The Lion and the Rose* he experiences in these two excerpts will leave him anticipating the rise of the next curtain and hoping that the intermission will soon be over. Our thanks to the composer for 20 minutes of excitement.

A lost art? In the century in which America ended up taking the operatic lead in number of new operas composed, the century that established English as the most common language for new operas? *The Lion and the Rose,* which was about as lowbrow as you could get and still be "elitist opera" had pretty much gone over his head, and these liner notes were the kind of thing you'd read in the programme book of a high school concert. It was rather unfortunate but the person who was determined to be Bill Middendorf's right-hand man was a person who only perceived one aspect of his vision.

For the rest of the SecNav's tenure in the Pentagon, McCracken managed to keep his nose mostly to the grindstone of the *marche militaire.*

Actually it was a huge burden lifted when it came to the military marches that now began flowing incessantly from the master's brain.

McCracken was a very adept band arranger with far more experience than I ever had or wanted. From that moment on, I no longer had to write full renditions of the marches; I could simply write out the melody, some harmonic indications or an important countermelody, and hand in a very much sketchier piece of paper which could then be arranged by Dick or perhaps one of the army of marine or navy arrangers to whom he had access.

In the end, for marches I'd only hand out the melody itself and a few chord symbols.

Why not? I was still getting $400 per march.

***

But my military adventures, perhaps, deserve a chapter of their own....

Chapter Eleven
An Intruder in the Pentagon

When I first visited the Middendorfs in their
Tobias Asserlaan home in the Hague, I didn't really
know the difference between a Democrat and a
Republican.   I just knew that they were political
parties, like the Tories and the Labour Party. I didn't
even realize that Bill was a Republican — a *big*
Republican.   I had heard whispers that he had
received his ambassadorship by donating a lot of
money to the Nixon campaign, but that just sounded
like the kind of thing we take for granted in Thailand,
where money trumps politics, and corruption trumps
everything.

My first inkling of this had come when I was
visiting the American School of the Hague and a
capmpaigner came around with buttons that said
VOTE FOR McGOVERN. They were a pretty color so

I took one, and later that evening I walked into the Middendorf household.

It was as Godzilla had emerged from the sea and the population of Tokyo were running, screaming, trampling each other underfoot.

It was finally Mrs. Middendorf who shouted, "Take that thing off!"

"The button?"

And Bill said, "You can't wear that in here ... he's ... he's the *Antichrist!*"

Later that evening, Bill apologized for the panic I had unwittingly caused. "I realize now, you just didn't know." I threw the button in the trash, which pleased him no end.

After arriving in America in the early 1970s, I would frequently be an uninvited guest inside the dark heart of the Republican Party. A fly on the wall, an unnoticed witness. Because Bill Middendorf was, if not God himself, at least a member of the innermost circle of Seraphim.

***

The SecNav now being ensconced in the Pentagon, a way had to be figured out for me to be able to work there. I wasn't an American citizen (at the time) and there was no way I could be awarded the kind of security clearance that would just let me walk in and out of the building. It would have been an unheard of breach of national security.

The next time I arrived in Washington, I was again driven to the house in McLean. The family came out to greet me and Isabelle and Amy rushed out, embraced me, and told me how delighted they were to see me.

I was taken aback. Mrs. Middendorf noticed and said, "It's all right, Somtow. I forgive you for everything. Jesus says I have to forgive people, and I do, sincerely."

"I see," I said. Silence fell. I could see I was expected to say something momentous. In the background, Bill was making encouraging gestures, like a prompter.

Suddenly I realized I was taking part in a Biblical psychodrama.

"Of course," I said. "I forgive you too."

Isabelle and Amy clasped their hands, rejoicing (the others looked a bit bored by the whole charade) and Bill looked extremely relieved indeed.

Of course, the mutual agape-fest did not extend to my actually staying as a guest in their house, so I was soon farmed out.

The first place they sent me to was to live in an apartment that was shared by three marines. I liked them a lot. They were completely alien to me in every way. I often didn't understand a word they were saying, and they were amazed I didn't drink, drive, or smoke like a chimney. And yet, their hospitality was boundless. For example, the freezer was constantly replenished with frozen TV dinners that I could make in the toast-r-oven. I realize now that Bill Middendorf was subsidizing this hospitality and yet they were very genuine and very generous.

Their friend was a female marine named Linda who, as it happened, was one of the SecNav's assistants. Linda did not fit my cliched preconception of what a marine should look like; she was petite, blonde, with an attractive perm. I don't recall her last name. She would not have looked out of place in one of those Hollywood beach movies.

Because I didn't have clearance, it was she who was despatched each day to pick me up at the Mall Entrance. She would then walk me through various corridors and escalators (The Pentagon, famously, is a building without lifts) and took me to the SecNav's office.

You can tell by the room number of every room in the Pentagon how to find it, because it's a building created with the utmost logic. I *think* the room I went to was called 4E-710 — but this *was* over forty years ago. If that was in fact the room number, you would go up the fourth floor, go to the E-ring and then the seventh corridor — you can see the logic. It was as ordered as a Bruckner symphony.

One passed a large waiting room and through various military staff before reach the outer chamber of the inner sanctum, which was ruled by a woman I would come to depend on over the next few years, Rita Fisher.

A small, relatively ample woman with — I think I recall — a page boy haircut and a New York accent, Rita Fisher had been with Bill Middendorf through thick and thin. She was the civilian in the room, but she was often also the adult. She was extremely loyal to Bill, and she knew what he really wanted before he even articulated it. She also understood how to get what he wanted, often without him knowing it. If I had had someone like her working with me for decades, I'd probably be a millionaire, too.

I daresay I am the only musical ghostwriter ever

to have an office in the Pentagon. They cleared out an old storeroom for me, and brought in a piano. The room had no windows. The lights were harsh.

In this coffin-like chamber, I sat day after day, banging out marches. When I had time, I also tried to compose for myself. But my two selves were definitely at war.

From time to time, I would be summoned to the SecNav's office. When I showed up, my priority topped everything. I remember people like Admiral Zumwalt being kept waiting outside while the SecNav, in his office, hummed enthusiastically and I took notes. I would wonder whether they were waiting for orders about what cities to bomb in Vietnam, or other dire deployments. At such times I would feel quite conflicted, but I told myself that surely the latest march could not possibly be holding up some military operation.

Once, when I left the office, I found myself taking a right instead of a left — I don't know why — and there was this back room. I was just looking at it when I was suddenly hustled out by men in uniform. Apparently I had occasioned some kind of security breach.

"You can't go back there," Bill said when I apologized for the accidental brouhaha. "There's a lot of top secret files."

I stayed away from the backroom from that moment on. Perhaps I had just escaped being arrested for espionage? Probably not. But it did occur to me that the Pentagon wasn't that secure.

Sometimes it was very lonely in there.

I would leave the little cubicle and walk around

aimlessly. The pentagon was structured in rings and corridors and impossible to get lost in once you knew the system, but it had miles and miles of hallways. Every so often there's be a a little room with vending machines, and you could heat up a little container of mac and cheese or cream of chicken soup.

I'd sit in those rooms, often as not completely alone, chowing down on classic American canned food. Occasionally I'd run into someone in a suit or a janitor and I would get stared at; not many people in the Pentagon had long hair, and in those days it wasn't very "equal-opportunity" — janitors were rarely white. Asians were rare, period.

***

At other times, I would be summoned, I think, because Bill needed a break from running the Navy.

Once, for example, I went into his office to discover about a hundred framed drawings propped up all the way round.

"Somtow," he said, "pick the ten ugliest of these drawings."

I took my time but I finally managed to pick what I considered rather undistinguished ones. He carefully put them to one side. Then he called someone to take them away.

He must have sensed my bewilderment, so he explained. He said, "I bought this entire sketchbook for a song, years ago. Now the individual pictures are worth a fortune. My tax advisor says I have to donate something to a museum and take a tax deduction."

"I see," I said. I didn't entirely see, but it was

clear that having an eye for cheap art could somehow make you save a lot of money on taxes years later. The museum, presumably, didn't have to know that it was the beneficiary of the "ten ugliest pictures" in the collection.

***

And then there were the marches.

I've already expounded a bit on Bill Middendorf's march-creating technique — one method was to start with a remembered theme and then change some of the notes.   Another that he liked very much was simply to repeat a note over and over.

For example ...

When you look at this on the page, you can't really imagine anything more boring, and this is what I thought when I heard him play it (yes, this is where the one-finger technique really came in useful.)

"No, no, you don't get it," he said. "Imagine just one trumpet playing. Then two, then three...."

Suddenly I realized what he meant. The second one coming in in thirds, maybe from the opposite side of the concert hall....

Then, maybe in triads with a third trumpet....
Musically, it is *nothing* ... yet if brilliantly played,

as indeed the Marine Band would, it could be very exciting. We spent a whole evening and I banged this out over and over, and Bill's excitement was infectious as he marched around the room, humming, waving his arms. "I'm going to call this *The Big Brass Band*," he said.   Eventually, when his album of marches came out, that was the title of the entire album.

Indeed, he rather convinced me on that one. His sense of drama, in this instance, was unfailing.

Drama also featured in *The Lollipop March,* which as far as I could tell, sounded a bit like the song "Long-haired Lover from Liverpool" by Jimmy Osmond.   As this was released in 1972, it was probably floating around in the ether.

It was a typically cute "children's" sort of melody and Bill had the outrageous idea of performing this with himself dressed as a bear, while children played the melody on kazoos.

Guess what! It worked. Lots of media attention and everyone admiring the *humanity* of this par-ticular SecNav.   Hundreds of children came to the event on the steps of the Jefferson Memorial and Bill had a glorious time chatting with them and he made all the news media.

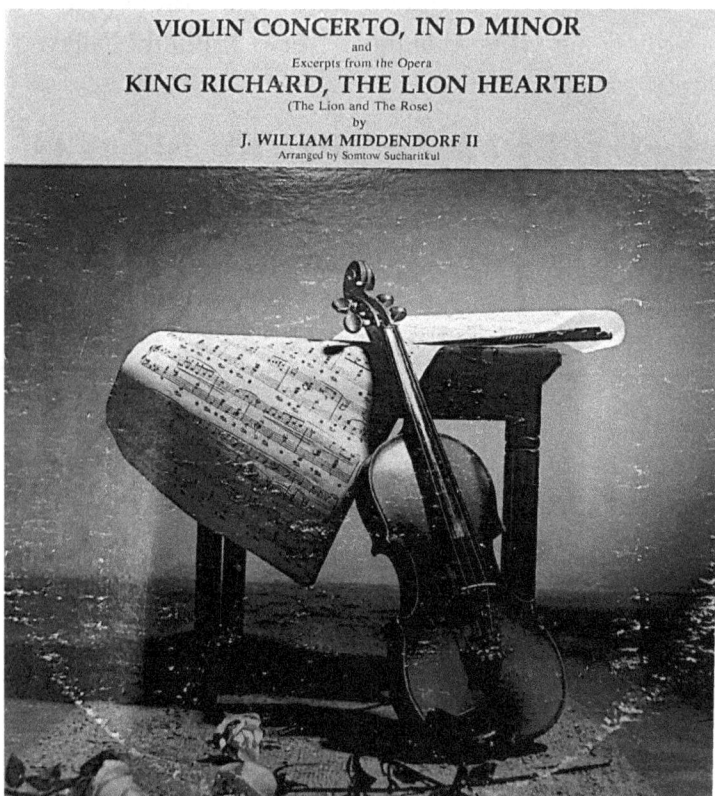

Violin Concerto • *Excerpts from* The Lion and the Rose • *LP*

So many marches. There were always a few spare marches in the drawer, so that if someone asked for a special new march, Bill could come up with one at the drop of a hat.

Eventually there was an LP of some of his favorites, including "Old Ironsides" which was premiered by the Boston Pops under Arthur Fiedler. Other major marches: The *Library of Congress March* I've mentioned, and then there was the *U.S. Capitol March* ... of which he said (to the Washington *Post*) "You know, no matter what foolishness we commit, we cannot kill the greatness that has been there."

He conducted it himself, too. He had learned how to do the gestures, and even managed to conduct a march with the St. Louis Symphony.

Indeed, Richard Hayman, pops conductor of that orchestra, had this to say about the Violin Concerto:

> "Here, indeed, is a concerto by an American composer that will hold an especially strong appeal for both performer and audience alike. This is due to the fact that it is a moving poetic work of intense romantic expression that demands of the soloist not only great virtuosity but also a warmth and elegance of style that causes an immediate effect on the listener's emotions. There is a breadth of soul in its themes...."

It is only now, several decades later, that I'm starting to get such ringing endorsements for my own music. Yet I am fully aware that if such a piece as these Middendorf compositions had come out under my name at the time, even if it could get performed at all, it would have been reviled as backward-looking, derivative claptrap. Indeed, had I heard one in a concert, *I* would have so reviled it, while perhaps grudgingly acknowledging that it was technically smoothly done.

***

So, during these Pentagon years, which lasted until Jimmy Carter was elected president, we fell into a routine. I would sometimes escape to New Haven, where I stayed with the Haggins, a family I loved very much (even though they lost my Chagall poster). In New Haven, I fell into another kind of routine: I would compose marches while watching afternoon sitcoms. *The Brady Bunch, Father Knows Best, That Girl,* were always in the background. I was a sucker for being manipulated by old TV shows; often I would find myself in tears at some dumb aphorism, wiping my eyes with my left while my right continued to place meticulous circles, dashes and tails on manuscript paper. I once found myself finishing a march on the plane on my way back to Washington.

Bill Middendorf paid for all those flights, and dozens of operas at the Met, and so much more. Then I'd fly to Tokyo to see my parents (not at Bill's expense — my Dad was on the board of now-defunct airline *Air Siam,* so as long as I could get to Los Angeles, I could get to Thailand, via Hawaii and Tokyo.) I'd spend a couple of weeks in Thailand, learning for the first time about many aspects of Thai culture that others in my family took for granted, and absorbing new musical influences from traditional music.

I moved from being housed with marines to an attic in the office of video company Smith-Mattingly Productions, whose owners had befriended me. After a while, though, they kicked me out because I didn't pick up after myself enough. The next time, I stayed in a service apartment-quasi-hotel called *Presidential*

Gardens, in a one-bedroom unit known as "Jefferson-D". It had an apple-green naugahyde sofa in a faux-colonial frame and lighting fixtures with eagles on them. This humble 500 square-foot box was my first real home, the first one I lived in all by myself. With the patient help of Betsy Mattingly, I learned how to drive. I purchased a gas-guzzling Pontiac. I started to feel pretty American. I started modifying my snooty Etonian accent, trying to ape the jazzy, sensual inflections of Standard American.

At Presidential Gardens, I leased-purchased a Selectric II of my very own (almost) and once in awhile, when feeling frustrated with the war between my two musical personalities, I would revisit my childhood by dashing off a science fiction story.

But more of science fiction in due course....

In California, I'd stay with friends I'd made in Europe, in particular the Frames who lived in Los Altos Hills; though they belonged to the same generally kooky church that Mrs. Middendorf was part of, they were beautiful people who tried their best to live a Christian life of giving and forgiving and plenty of love. The matriarch of this family, Héloise, was one of the most genuinely decent people I ever met. They, and many other people I met in these trips to the States — the Smit family whose paterfamilias was Bill Middendorf's accountant — all of them welcomed me warmly and showed me a way of life I'd never seen before — one where people didn't lock their homes, welcomed surprise guests to dinner with open arms, listened wide-eyed to curious anecdotes about the mystic east — for the early 1970s was a time when Americans were open and openminded and were not wary of strangers.

I fell in love with America, with its vastness, with its "anything is possible" attitudes. I resolved that I would move to America permanently as soon as I could. Before that, however, I really needed to absorb everything I could from my own culture, from which I had been alienated since being carried off to England at the age of six months....

***

The time had come for me to take another brief trip to Asia; my parents' posting in Japan was coming to an end, and I received a letter from something that called itself the Bangkok Opera Society, inviting me to become its music director for 1977. This would give me a real reason to spend a few months in Thailand. A chance to give my other self — Other-Somtow — a chance.

My two identities had been at loggerheads since I was the moment I stepped into No. 4, Tobias Asserlaan. I told myself, *You have to decide whether to be Peter Schickele or P.D.Q. Bach.* If given time to develop and grow, could the dog ever wag its tail, or was the dog doomed to be wagged for all time by a tail — and not exactly its own tail at that?

Little did I know that it would take a few decades to totally untangle that metaphor....

Chapter Twelve
An Intermezzo in Bangkok

The intermezzo in Bangkok: this wasn't a tidy "movement of a symphony". It overlapped with what you have already read, and its tendrils stretch into upcoming chapters. But it's a defining line in my life. It's where the war between the two Somtows came to a head. Afterwards, the relationship between Bill Middendorf and me would never be quite the same, because the Other-Somtow came of age.

The story of those brief years is really another book in itself, with the Other-Somtow as its narrator. I will just touch on the highlights.

I started with short trips to Thailand. I was seen

as a bit of curiosity.   There wasn't a truly "Thai" classical music scene, but there were many very active ex-pats.   These people had created the Bangkok Opera Society, the Bangkok Music Group, and many other organizations that were run by an assortment of eccentrics, from people temporarily posted in Thailand because of the embassy or of working for a multinational, or those who had "gone native" and were living their dream lives, often surrounded with a collection of attractive and adoring little brown things when in their own countries they probably would not have been viewed as particularly attractive.

The Bangkok Opera Society had lured me with the promise of conducting *Dido and Aeneas,* but on my arrival I discovered it had been converted into *Amahl and the Night Visitors.*   In fact, it may have been flattering to be invited to fly in and be music director, but in fact the job had been palmed off on my by one Bruce Gaston.

Bruce Gaston, who was the son of a preacher in Pasadena, who had played Beethoven's First Piano Concerto with Zubin Mehta at the age of twelve, who was Michael Tilson Thomas's room mate in college, had come to Thailand, perhaps to escape the draft, perhaps to learn about Thai music — or both.   But he was more knowledgeable, and more articulate, about Thai classical music than most of the Thai people I knew.   Perhaps it was because he was able to explain its structures to me in terms I could understand with my western education.   He also spoke much better Thai than I did.

Dnu Huntrakul had studied in Holland and Oregon and had recently returned to Thailand.   He, too, spoke better Thai than I.

These two very colorful personalities were soon working with me and there ensued a period of musical ferment, a dramatic flowering, that pretty much turned the music scene in Thailand on its ear.

We soon teamed up with some of the most colorful personalities in Bangkok.   Dr. Anton Regenberg was the head of the Goethe Institute in Bangkok, and he plunged headlong into helping us to build a genuine national school of contemporary music, where we could move freely between the sounds and structures of Southeast Asian music and the latest contemporary techniques.

Nop Sotthibhandu, a self-taught violinist who believed himself to be the reincarnation of Vishnu, or Krishna, or one of those other many-headed Indian gods, had an incredible imagination though little formal training in composition. Veeraphan Vawklang was a violinist who was one of the first to receive a full European training. Witaya Tumornsoontorn was a musical enthusiast who put together the Bangkok Chamber Orchestra, which would become an ancestor of the Bangkok Symphony.   Young artist Chatvichai Prohmadattavedi was in charge of the newly created Bhirasri Institute, where all sorts of modern art was being created and displayed.

Piyabhand Sanitwong, a pianist and aristocrat who had once come second in the Leeds piano competition, hosted all these wild people in his living room, which had a Bösendorfer and the largest collection of LPs I had ever seen.

Chronicling all this madness was perhaps the most intellectual person I have ever known, Bob

Halliday. A journalist who worked for the Bangkok
Post, Bob spoke fluently dozens of languages, like
Cambodian and Hungarian. He kept a full score of
Lulu under his pillow and he could complete *any*
phrase I sang to him from Berg's *Wozzeck.* He was a
member of a world wide James Joyce society that
spent its time analyzing *Finnegans Wake* and arguing
about its interpretation.

One of the most important financiers of the
movement was the Ford Foundation, headed in
Thailand by the late Peter Geithner. His eldest son,
Tim, whom we would later know as the Secretary of
the Treasurer under President Obama, was 15. His
twin sons, David and Jonathan, were different as
night and day, but I met them through the 12-year-old
David who played the rôle of Amahl in my
production of Menotti's opera. Peter had a lovely,
sensitive daughter named Sarah and his wife Deborah
was an extraordinary woman: intelligent, warm, a
brilliant pianist (years later she played the *Goldberg
Variations* in Carnegie Hall) who opened their home
on Soi 7 to me, allowing me to compose a magnum
opus on their dining room table.

Patron of the movement was the feisty Princess
Chumbhot, widow of Prince Chumbhot of Nagor
Svarga, known for her arty parties at the Suan Pakkad
Palace. Possessor of an almost parody-like upper
crust British accent, she would have dinners where
she served such endangered species as sea-turtles, or
inventive recipes such as noodles with escargot butter.
Once, she dropped me off at an ice cream parlor with
Princess Micaëla von Habsburg, perhaps trying to set

up something. Under the Thai system of nobility, Princess Chumbhot was not actually a princess, since wives do not automatically acquire their husband's status. She was, however, an aristocrat of high noble standing, a Mom Rajawongse of the Devakula Branch, directly descended from King Rama IV.

A story about Princess Chumbhot, which perhaps sums up Thailand in this period in a nutshell, was told by Bob Halliday:

He told me that when he first arrived in Thailand, he had been invited to lunch at Suan Pakkad Palace. Over an exquisite meal, the Princess told Bob that she didn't care about the trappings of aristocracy. "As far as I'm concerned, let the communists come. I don't mind being abolished and living in an egalitarian society!"

At that moment, an aged servant entered the room to serve tea, crawling on her hands and knees and arthritically working her way toward the dining table.

"But surely, Princess," Bob said, "how can you say these things when you have servants crawling around on the floor?"

She replied, "If you have to ask such a question, Bob, you will never understand Thailand."

This indeed was a central paradox at the heart of the culture, a heady blend of futurism and feudalism, where opposite realities could simultaneously be true.

I learned as much from my new peers in Thailand as I had learned from my fellow-students in Cambridge. Bruce taught me about the joys of being foul-mouthed as well as many secrets of traditional Thai music.

This fledgling movement put on events at a frenetic pace. The co-composed *Hexaphony* was 90 minutes of structured improvisation which toured in the newly built Cultural Center of the Philippines. Bruce wrote a groundbreaking opera, *Chuchok,* for which the Goethe Institute brought in an avant-garde German director. Dnu and I founded the Temple of Dawn Consort, the first contemporary music ensemble. My piece *Gongula* for Thai and Western instruments was so controversial that the Thai instrumentalists went on strike — and much of this unorthodox activity was chronicled in the main-stream press and on television.

Indeed, the first piece I ever wrote in the full Other-Somtow vein, *Views from the Golden Mountain,* received a sterling review from a caller who rang the station in mid-broadcast, telling the station that a dog had started howling when my music was playing and that she thought it was part of the piece.

To cut a long story short, the whole revolution culminated in March, 1978 with the "Asian Composers Expo 78" hosted by the newly formed Thai Composers Association and such big sponsors as UNESCO, Ford Foundation, Goethe Institute ... and many generous individuals.

However, it was also perfectly clear that the musical establishment hated my guts.

At a rooftop reception at Toni Regenberg's home, a famous Thai pianist started screaming at me about how I was bringing all these "foreign influences" to Thailand. "How can you say that?" I responded. "Aren't you sitting around playing Tchaikovsky and

Chopin? Aren't *they* foreign?" She spluttered and didn't speak to me for twenty years.

At the opening of *Amahl and the Night Visitors,* the leading soprano's driver marched up to me after the dress rehearsal and started cussing me out. "How *dare* you have Thai dances and musicians in the middle of this production! You are polluting our culture!" he screamed as I put up my hands to avoid being punched in the face.

As the Expo began, one of Thailand's leading newspapers wrote a long editorial about it. Basically their message to us was that this was a hopelessly over-intellectual exercise that would never reach the public.

It was the Department of Fine Arts, in those days part of the Ministry of Education rather than its own ministry, that reacted most weirdly. The opening concert was to feature the premiere of *Gongula III,* one of my rather innovative pieces, and a performance by Boonyong Ketkhong, the leading composer of Thai traditional music (who had not yet received the official imprimatur of acceptance from the department.)

On the afternoon of the concert, I went up to the podium and discovered that the piano had been spirited away.

"They've stolen the piano!" I screamed. The rehearsal could not begin.

Finally a bureaucrat came down from the department to inform me that the piano had been removed. "We have scientifically determined that modern music will harm the strings of the piano, and have removed it for its protection."

Because the piano part was essential, and this was the opening night to which two hundred delegates from different Asian countries were coming, plus famed Americans like Robert Ashley. this would have caused the entire movement to fizzle in embarrassment.

The Goethe Institute came to the rescue. They sent the aging Ibach piano from the institute on the back of a truck (an open-backed truck with the piano lashed to the sides with rope — very scary — but in 1978 the only way to deliver a piano was with a company named 'Hoe San' — and this truck.)

The concert was saved by the skin of its teeth.

And I was pretty much burned out.

Other-Somtow had tried existing without his alter ego for over a year.

Post partum, and the venomous hatred of those who had felt "left out" of things, had gotten to me. I felt that all my cherished ambitions had crashed and burned.

I didn't talk to anyone. Princess Chumbhot had a huge celebratory dinner and I simply didn't — *couldn't* — go. I simply could face any more of it.

I quietly snuck away, back to America.

***

Now, J. William Middendorf, II had not been entirely absent from my existence during this intermezzo. I did have to pop into the U.S. once in a while, even though marches were not exactly raining from my pen.

There was, for example. the ill-fated *Bicentennial Symphony* — his sixth entry in the symphonic genre.

This was a pretty ambitious work and had a chorus, like Beethoven's Ninth.   I think there were five movements, but I only remember the last two clearly.

The second-last movement began with a chorus singing in bare fifths the words "fourscore and seven years ago."   The phrases echoed back and forth against a tremolando high string background … much like the second movement of Mahler's *Symphony of a Thousand.*

The final movement had a fugue sung to the words "One nation under God."   It was one of those very stately fugues, kind of like the fugue "Herr, du bist würdig" from the Brahms *Requiem.*

The *Bicentennial* was Bill Middendorf's most ambitious symphony to date and he longed to have it performed.

Some friends of mine, the Hong family, were New York Chinese who also lived in Taipei, where the wife, Florence, taught at Soo Chow University and had dual citizenship. She arranged for a premiere of the symphony in Taiwan. The chorus was learning the music and a lot of effort was being expended to make it possible.

However, in the end, the U.S. government would not allow Bill Middendorf to travel to Taiwan, even as a private citizen, to go to this premiere. After all, this wasn't long after the whole "Nixon in China" initiative, and in order to recognize China, the United States had to un-recognize Taiwan as the "real" China.

We ourselves had the same problem with the Asian Composers Expo 78. When UNESCO came on board, they invited China, meaning the entire

Taiwan contingent was forced to boycott the event.

For Bill it was the first time that his government position was actually thwarting his music: most of the time, it was an asset, enabling him to get all sorts of works performed, and opening all sorts of doors.

My long absence was quite frustrating to Bill's creative passions; whenever I wasn't around, he tried to work through other amanuenses. His most successful work not passing through my hands at any point was perhaps the song *Stand Up for America* which emerged in the Bicentennial year, 1976, a time in which my absences from Washington were starting to increase. A survey of the Middendorf marches available for sale from various publishers has a number of names I don't recognize, so I am not quite sure how many of these marches bypassed me altogether. Because my delivery of marches was only in short score, or sometimes just in melody and chord symbols, I couldn't be said to have meaningfully "arranged" them, but sometimes, during the Pentagon days, I had managed to derive a lot of thematic material from very little humming — sometimes only a bar or two — after all, a Sousa-like march tune can be generated from virtually any sequence of a few notes.

    ***

In the spring of 1978, however, I was back in the States. The Other-Somtow — creator of controversial and uncompromisingly modern music — seems to have shot his wad. The Sausage-Factory Somtow, however, still had a few sausages left to squeeze out.

By all accounts, Bill Middendorf was a very

effective SecNav; he must have been, because Jimmy Carter asked him to stay on. He demurred and, as the Democratic Party took over the government for the next four years, he went back to the private sector and was connected to some huge multinational financial project. I believe it was called First American.

Chapter Thirteen
A Symphony in McLean

Between the avant-garde composer and the musical hack, a third Somtow was starting to emerge. I've said that sometimes the identity conflict was so stressful that I'd take a break and dash off a science fiction story. In 1977, I popped into a science fiction convention in the Hunt Valley Inn, in the area around Baltimore. I met a lot of writers I admired when I was a child, and got my first experience of the fans — what an interesting bunch they were! — argumentative, consciously elitist, very very bright, very very geek-like, with their own secret language, underground publications, and cliquish camaraderie. I felt very much at home, as someone who had felt "different" since childhood. They were people who actually seemed to understand and accept my various weirdnesses.

At this convention I met two young men from Boston, John Landsberg and Jonathan Ostrowsky-Lantz. They were editing a magazine called *Unearth,* dedicated to previously undiscovered writers. I asked them if I could contribute something. They said, "Sure, why not?" and I drove all the way back to Arlington, Virginia, to fetch a story from my files, and then back the same night to hand it to them.

They sent me a check, and used it in their very next issue. My story "Sunsteps" shared an issue with the first published by stories by William Gibson (whose novel "Neuromancer" would later give birth to the cyberpunk movement) and James P. Blaylock. It is quite a collector's item today.

On my return to Washington in 1978, my third alter ego, the science fiction writer, began to assert himself more and more. This was especially since I felt my entire efforts in Southeast Asia had been a dismal failure.

***

Over the next few years I only produced a few pieces of what I would think of as "real music", and each of them had some connection with science fiction. The neo-Asian-post-serialist was becoming the Thai-sci-fi writer.

Through my science fiction fan friend Suzy Koon, who worked in an office by day but doubled as a belly dancer named Jamielah by night, I'd found a place to live in Arlington; I was renting the basement of an entrepreneur named Reid Hartsell, who hailed from

Emporia, Virginia, where, he assured me, "everybody" was a member of the Klan.

While Reid frequently inveighed against blacks, orientals, and so on in Archie Bunker-like tones, he never once let on that he might have thought I was a member of any lower order.   Indeed he was an uncommonly decent and good-hearted person. There was a complete disconnect between how he actually treated me, and the cliches of KKK-speak which occasionally spewed forth. I never saw him associate with any member of a minority except myself, so perhaps he never noticed I was one.

My return to America meant frequent Middendorf sessions.   His preferred place to work was an upper room of the Army and Navy Club. It was there that his Seventh Symphony took shape.

The Seventh was like a highly condensed Mahler symphony, especially the last movement.   It had a pretty, lilting scherzo with a lot of woodwind passages in sixths, a soul-searching if brief slow movement, and a rousing finale — with excruciatingly high violin parts, which I soon was to learn were actually beyond the capabilities of amateur string players.

And soon I was to meet the man who would conduct this work: the director of the McLean Symphony, a man with the delightful name of Dingwall Fleary.

McLean (a rich suburb, as I have mentioned) boasted its own symphony, a mostly volunteer group who performed at the Alden Theater in the local community center.

Dingwall was a fine musician. He was the only African American person for miles around in that neighborhood, except for his wife and son. Yet he was adept at manipulating the tycoons, politicians, CIA operatives and diplomats who inhabited McLean.

Dingwall had a resonant deep voice and spoke in an accent that sounded a little Caribbean. The McLean Symphony had been in existence only briefly at that point, and was looking to premiere a work by its local celebrity, the politician, diplomat and business wizard — for Bill Middendorf represented, in a single person, the entire demographic of his town.

Dingwall Fleary

At first, we were trying to get "Ding" to do the Bicentennial Symphony, but the work was a bit too large in scope. So we missed another opportunity to do the Sixth, which is unperformed to this day.

The Seventh, newly created, seemed ideal and it was soon in rehearsal.

I learned a few practical things that year. First, I'd always composed instrumental parts with the assumption that people could play *anything*. The Cambridge musicians had done little to dissuade me from that notion. They actually *could* play anything, or if not, could fake it so brilliantly that no one noticed.

But the McLean musicians showed me that it was fine to sound like Mahler, but not fine to be as difficult as Mahler.

Dingwall ruthlessly dropped the more strato-spheric string parts an octave to make them able to play. He simplified horn parts. Presently, No. 7 started to sound very respectable.

But — as Paul Webster had told me when we were recording the excerpts from *The Lion and the Rose* — the music was "getting to me."

As a knowledgable musician *and* as somehow who knew the principals involved, Dingwall was one of the only people in the U.S. that I could speak to frankly about the Middendorf collaboration and my own feelings of self-doubt and identity confusion. He always listened and always understood my dilemma. And this convinced me that I should get up and say something to Bill about my feelings.

It was at this time that I wrote a soul-searching letter to Bill Middendorf....

***

I'm paraphrasing now, but the letter basically said, "Bill, I'm *tired*." I had already created more or less an entire oeuvre: concertos, symphonies, an opera, and dozens of marches.   After allowing my repressed "real" self to come back, I'd been beaten back by the musical establishment of Thailand and and returned to the States in a huge depression, feeling that I had accomplished very little in life.   I poured out my frustration and confessed about being torn between these warring personalities.

I asked Bill if I could be allowed to slow down a bit — to have time to "find myself" as it were.   He was, as always, very sympathetic.

"Sure," he said, "you must take a break."

But I didn't really take one, not right away. Although Bill was still paying generously for my work, I was now actually living in America rather than a guest, a visitor, so I wasn't having my accommodation paid for anymore.   There wasn't any room service at Reid's basement.   I had become a freelancer, living hand to mouth, and I truly needed the work.

However, within a few months of my return to America, I started reaping the rewards of what had really only been a sort of therapeutic exercise, writing science fiction stories; within a week of each other, I sold a story, *The Thirteenth Utopia,* to *Analog* magazine, and another story, *A Day in Mallworld,* to *Isaac Asimov's Science Fiction Magazine.*

As my "serious composer" personality receded into the background, a "sci-fi" personality was emerging to take its place.

The science fiction was deeply satisfying because it was my own work and in a sense "honest" work. I found myself selling more stories, thanks to the team at *Asimov's* magazine which was looking for writers who appealed to their particular sensibility, and having found them, remained loyal to them. On one occasion I had the "cover story" at *Asimov's* several issues in a row. George Scithers, the editor, was a military man himself. Now that he has passed away I think we can say that he was a somewhat closeted military man. He cultivated a very special tone at the magazine, somewhat retro in looking back to the "Golden Age" of science fiction and meticulous avoiding the more nebulous, literary "New Wave" style that had arisen in the mid 1960s. These were stories with beginnings, middles and ends, clear conflicts, well-defined characters, and more or less believable science.

For a musician, it was a very easy market to write for because such stories are structured very much like short pieces of music: theme, secondary theme, development section, climax, coda … it really took only a tiny sidewise motion to become more and more adept. And, while it took longer to write a $400 short story than a $400 march, it was my own name on it, and I was reaching out to people whose world-view matched my own, and being sucked into a community in which being different was the norm.

***

At the premiere of the Seventh Symphony, I slightly lost my self-control.

Ever since all this began, I had often been asked the question, sometimes with a snicker, sometimes in genuine bewilderment: "He didn't *really* compose this, did he?"

Since it was a question I could barely answer for myself, I usually tried to answer the question in a noncommittal way. Well actually, no. I usually avoided discussion by just saying "Yes." And, if drawn into further discussion about my actually rôle, I'd talk about the art of arranging.

There was a reception after the premiere of the Seventh and Bill was going around beaming and accepting people's compliments.

I was standing around wolfing down the finger food.

A small group of the McLean upper crust – well fed, well-dressed, balding — were chatting nearby. When they saw me, one of them said, "Aren't you the arranger?"

"Yes."

"So tell us — we know Bill Middendorf and doesn't strike us as being that musical. But this symphony is a gem! It's brilliantly orchestrated! It hangs together really well! Surely he didn't do all that himself?"

Hearing all those compliments, I couldn't resist confessing: "Well, I did have a rôle."

"Yes but how much of a rôle?"

"Well … I orchestrated it."

"That's all?" This person was kind of insistent, and I am not a good drinker, but I'd had some.

"Well, I sort of assembled it from his sketches," I said, trying to sound proud and humble simultaneously.

"He has sketches?" said our would-be critic, whom I was starting to suspect might be a member of the board of the McLean Symphony. "What I'd give to see one of those sketches! What do they look like? How detailed are they, how much of the harmony and counterpoint is in them, or do you have to come up with all of that yourself?"

The die was cast.   "Well, it's sort of ... humming," I explained.

I realized that I had been tricked or cajoled into revealing "the secret," such as it was. My conversationalist began laughing. I wondered whether I had accidentally ruined the whole evening.

***

But my inability to keep entirely mum came to a head because of the science fiction community. A well known editor named Ted White, who put together *Amazing Stories* from his house in Falls Church, got me talking, and I was more voluble that was wise. I kept saying, don't print this, don't print that, and he said, "Oh don't worry, I wouldn't print anything that would hurt you."

Imagine my horror when the exposé came out. It was a whole page in — I think *City Paper* — the weekly that everyone used to get in order to find out what movies were on where.

Much of the article dealt with how I fallen into a septic tank in Bangkok — indeed that was one of my most bizarre adventures the last time I had been there.

It also talked about my ghost-writing all of Bill Middendorf's work and it was certainly a sort of hatchet job. Every now and then he would hark back to the septic tank story — I had recently written about that in a fanzine that I created along with a 14-year-old literary prodigy named Dan Joy. (Later, Dan would enter a long period of being stoned all the time, and he and I sort of drifted apart.) I should also mentioned Jack Lechner, a friend of Dan's, who was later to become a big Hollywood producer. At the time, though, he was producing a xeroxed fanzine called *Vorpal Sword,* which actually published my first (nonprofessional) short story. He also made a monster movie in 8-millimeter called *Tokyo Shoeshine Boy,* in which I played all the roles (of both sexes) — the idea being that "they all look alike". But I digress.

Ted White — the first hatchet job

The article in the City Paper was really the most

bizarre article. Witty in a barbed sort of way. And quite viciously out to get Bill Middendorf, who was I suppose not much liked by people on the liberal side of the political spectrum. It quoted me, about my feelings — which at the time were about the same as I'd stated in the letter I wrote Bill, the rather despairing letter in which I had asked if I could get some time off or slow down.

The next time I went to see Bill, the mood was awkward. He had the paper on his desk. He had a look, not of anger, but of disappointment, sorrow ... betrayal. He looked like I'd punched him in the solar plexus.

He said to me, "Do you really feel this way about our work?"

How was I to answer? There *was* a part of me that felt that way. But definitely not *all* of me. There was a part that was really into this work, the challenges, the technical aspect, learning more and more about my craft from doing the work and actually hearing it performed by real musicians — even the audacity of it, the secret pleasure of pulling one over on the audience.

Bill went on, "If you don't feel good about this, if you don't really *want* to do it anymore ... I don't mind. I can find another way."

The sadness in his voice was — in its way — heartrending.

A part of me said to myself, This is a good time to end it. Maybe Ted shouldn't have written the article, but maybe it was a good thing because it forces the issue. I *have* to get up and say, okay, this is not me.

At that moment, I had it in my power to walk

away. Okay I would lose a major source of income, but I would be free, full time, to finally discover who I really was.

But the *sadness....*

Bill Middendorf had a genuine vision. Maybe he didn't have the technical ability to bring this vision about, but the passion was real. The sadness was real. I had been working with Bill, on and off, for seven or eight years by now. I'd seen what music meant to him. In a sense, he had the soul of a composer. In his darkest moments, music was his light.

I just couldn't walk away just yet, although I knew now that it would one day be inevitable. Because there was a quest I too had to pursue. There was a journey I had to make, and this journey did not include any travelling companions. And my time was running out. But not quite yet.

So I said, "Bill ... these journalists ... they love to twist everything you say."

The relief on his face was immediate.

"I knew you didn't mean to say those things," he said, smiling broadly. "Let's get back to work."

Chapter Fourteen
An Ellis Island of the Mind

Having escaped from what I saw as a closed-minded, hostile environment, I really wanted to drop my anchor in America. I had told Bill Middendorf that I wanted to find a way to stay longer than a few months at a time, and he immediately told me he would find a way to arrange it.

Sometime before Ted White's bubble-bursting article in the Washington paper, my "friend in a high place" had already been looking for some kind of special dispensation to allow me to immigrate to the United States. It wouldn't really do for him to simply hire me officially to write symphonies under his name, after all. Not the kind of job offer expected in a visa application.

My being in the United States at that time was a little irregular. I had a diplomatic passport, because my father was an ambassador. My visa was a G-2, meaning that I was part of my father's entourage — he had business at the U.N. from time to time. It felt a little insecure. If my sources of income dried up, I wouldn't be able to even get a job flipping burgers.

Bill Middendorf had many, many contacts, of course, both as a businessman and as a high-ranking government person. His first thought was to make me a U.S. citizen by an act of congress.

This may seem outlandish, but it fact, I was told, it was done more often than one thought. It was something called a private bill. I think that a number of prominent foreigners became American in this way.

Bill Middendorf asked his close advisor Robert Ferneau to look into it, but apparently there weren't any slots like that, or any senators that needed a favor in return at that moment. Instead, Ferneau offered to take me to be interviewed by someone at the very top of the food chain. I asked him who that was but his only response was, "She's black."

He expected me to be impressed, or astounded, at this fact, and all the way to this lady's office he regaled me with tales of the sexual talents of African American women, opining that the super-sized ones were the best. "In fact," he told me, "I have one I see on a regular basis. She is *huge*. She is just the best lay you can imagine. You really have to try it."

My imagination was not going there that day.

In fact, in those days I found "locker room talk" to be a bit unnerving. I don't know whether the woman we were about to go and see was equated in Ferneau's mind with the "huge" creature of his love life. What I found disturbing as well was how he casually spoke of en entire group of people as being not entirely human.

Later, as I actually started living in America, my idealistic vision of America as a melting-pot of egalitarian-minded people devoid of prejudices began to erode. I think this moment of guy talk was when I started to notice it.

Now that I think about it, he was probably trying to bond with me and make me less nervous, but by the time we got to this lady's office I was a wreck.

However, the lady was incredibly nice. She looked through the information we had brought — "Cambridge master's ... successful musician ... has already published stories ..." She said, "You're exactly the kind of person we want to immigrate to the United States. Here's a form, just fill it out and hand it in downstairs. It'll come up to me for approval."

What a lovely person! I thought. I have been trying to figure out who she is, lately, because although she was introduced to me as the "head" of immigration, I recently looked up the past holders of the top immigration position and could not discover anyone matching the woman I met.

I quickly filled out the form and took it downstairs.

The lady behind the counter was another African American woman, but this one was quite different from the one I'd just met. She was one of those bureaucrats toiling in a dull job in which the only moments of pleasure came from wielding power over some hapless supplicant.

"You can't hand that in here," she said.

I said, "But I've just seen" — the lady in question whose name I cannot remember now — "and she said to hand it in, and it would go up to her so she would approve it."

"It don't matter what the lady upstairs say," she said to me. "Down here, I'm the only one that count. You don't get pass me, you don't get approval."

Bewildered, I asked her what else I needed.

"You need a labour certification," she said. "It says here, you a writer."

"A science fiction writer," I said.

"Well, you go on down to the labour department and get me a paper that say that the job of science fiction writer is not one that is being taken away from an American, and then you come back and hand in that form."

I pointed to the back of the form where there was a paragraph listing the occupations that were specifically excluded from needing a labour certification, including the occupation of "writer."

"It don't matter what the form say," she said. "It only matter what *I* say."

Although I was bewildered and frustrated, I have to note that this was the first time I had ever had an extended conversation with someone who spoke this particular dialect. To me, not having grown up with the prejudices that underlay American society, it was something melodious and had its own lilting beauty and energy.   Later on I was to become very much drawn to this culture-within-a-culture, and it came to have a great influence over several of my books and stories, notably the horror novel *Darker Angels* and my semi-autographical novel *Jasmine Nights*.

Right now, however, I was faced with the problem of how to hand in the form at the counter.

It ended up taking me six years to hand in that form.

***

After the Seventh Symphony, it seemed that Bill was a little bit symphonied out.   But a number of unusual works did come into existence during that time.

For example, there was this ballet, *Cinderella*. Scored for just two pianos, I believe that it was originally composed for a school ballet — or a ballet school, I'm not sure which, now.   I do not believe it was ever performed.

It has a lot of charm, and would be easy enough to do.   The piano parts are not hard, either.   Students could manage them easily.

Unfortunately the first movement is all I can locate in my files.   This has been one of the most difficult parts of assembling this memoir; I didn't keep copies, and now I am half a world away.

Bill never essayed another symphony.   I think that shorter pieces delivered more instant gratification, so most of the rest of his oeuvre would tend to be shorter, snappier, and concentrating on a single image or idea.

Excerpt from Cinderella, *a ballet, for two pianos, in Somtow's hand*

There were also, of course, more marches, because Bill Middendorf was becoming known as — if not the March King, an honour that belonged permanently to John Phillip Sousa — at the very least a minor Duke or Count. How many marches were there? I myself lost count but I found a xerox in my files which is marked #117. The numbering is in Bill Middendorf's own hand, but the title and the musical notation is in mine.

March ms. with numbering in Middendorf's hand

This would imply that there are at least 117 marches extant in some form or another, whether as sketches, like the one above, in short score, or in complete band arrangements by third parties.

As you can see, the above just bare bones. It's possible that there are dozens more somewhere. A google search for published marches shows around a dozen or so that a concert band could order and put in their programme. Others, presumably, remain unpublished, were produced only *ad occasionem*, or exist in the form of sketches such as the one I found in my files.

My trusty Wikipedia informs me that Sousa wrote 137 marches. The one I found in my files was undoubtedly *not* J. William Middendorf's last, so it is not out of the question that in sheer quantity, Middendorf and I may have given Sousa a real run for his money.

***

I tried reading up on the immigration laws and discovered that if I could convince them that I was a person with unique skills in the arts or sciences, I could qualify for a thing called "third preference" and cut short the queue a bit for that green card. So I made another attempt.

This time, I knew I needed to get a few fulsome letters from celebrities stating how qualified I was, so I got to work, starting with Bill himself. Presently I got a small stack of such letters including one from Peter Geithner of the Ford Foundation which stated that I was "one of the few persons I have known to legitimately be possessed of genius" — a bit overblown if one took the Middendorf oeuvre as representative, but one assumed that the folks at U.S. Immigration were not music critics.

I went to the place myself, hoping not to have another confrontation with the all-powerful woman who had told me that only what *she* said counted.

I took a book to read because I thought it would take a long time. The book was *Shogun.* Even though I am a fast reader, I thought *Shogun* would be long enough to last however long I needed to wait. I got there really early in the morning, anticipating several hours in line. I registered and waited for my name to be called. I got through a good three quarters of the book —

By 4 pm, my name hadn't yet been called. I had been to the toilet once, but surely it couldn't have been called then. Everyone who had been there when I first arrived, however, was no longer there.

I now suspect that the person calling names just didn't want to go to the trouble of trying to pronounce my name.

Anyway, as closing time approached, I decided to

to go up the counter and just pretend my name had been called.   They didn't question it, took the paperwork. I didn't know how long I'd have to wait, but at least one stage was out of the way.

The main problem was, I wasn't really supposed to leave the country until they answered, so I settled down to what I thought would be a few months of alternating Middendorf and science fiction.

Science fiction began taking up more time.   I became more involved in the entire world, from conventions to fanzines; since I was now eligible to join the Science Fiction Writers of America, I was getting to know pretty much everyone in this close-knit world, from Isaac Asimov on down.

And thus it was that, using science fiction as a catalyst, the Other-Somtow made a last-ditch attempt to set the agenda.   Invited to perform music the International Conference on the Fantastic in Boca Raton, Florida, I wove together lyrics in an invented language that I'd created for one of those galaxy-spanning space opera trilogies, with contemporary music techniques, and came up with a song cycle that was premiered by the Florida Atlantic Contemporary Music Ensemble — which consisted of music students recruited by their somewhat reluctant music director, John Hutchcroft.

Although they didn't go as far as to hide the piano, putting on this work was, in microcosm, as traumatic as the festival opening concert in Thailand had been.   Again, "Other-Somtow" will probably write his own book one of these days, so let us just say that all this reinforced my feeling that expressing my true self had a tendency to result in too much mental anguish.

Mind you, it was great to have so many fine fantasists be around to hear one's composition, from Stephen King to Fritz Leiber to Brian Aldiss to legendary editor David Hartwell. Barry Malzberg, a writer noted for being depressed a lot and writing very depressing fiction, played the second violin in my piece and smiled all the way through, later claiming that I was "just like Ozawa," though I think this had as much to do with being an Asian with long hair as any conducting skills I may have had at the time.

***

No, it was safer to sit around writing marches. And in this period there were other, more interesting pieces as well; there was an overture reminiscent of the music for the film *The Sea Hawk;* there was a set of variations for piano and orchestra that recapitulated the history of music.

And yet, even though these orchestral pieces were technically more well done than what we had done in Holland, I didn't feel as much joy in the process anymore. Sometimes I'd fill five hours of cassettes with my improvising and Bill's humming, deep into the night at the Army and Navy Club, and I'd be able to pick through those hummings and get out a couple of months' worth of compositions. I have to admit, as well, that the immigration thing was a constant underlying stress. I yearned to be able go out and get real jobs from time to time.

By 1980, however, I'd sold a novel to Simon and Schuster (it would come out in 1981) and the list of short stories was growing.

One day there came a letter from the Immigration and Naturalization Service. Full of trepidation, I opened it.

My application had been rejected, and I had two weeks to leave the country voluntarily.

***

Now, as it happened, I didn't leave.

When I showed the letter to someone at the Thai embassy, they said, "What are you worried about? You have a diplomatic passport. Your normal visa hasn't expired, and even if it had, you have immunity."

Somehow this wasn't that comforting. I had nightmares about being dragged off in the middle of the night by La Migra ... yet, nothing actually happened to me.

However, the curious partnership of Middendorf and Somtow still had an Indian summer left. There was to be a final outpouring of music.

It happened because Jimmy Carter was only a one-term president; thus, J William Middendorf, II, was perforce a one-term tycoon, for Ronald Reagan and the Republican Party called once again. At first, Bill had some duties that had something to do with the CIA. I know what he really wanted was to be Secretary of Defense, but it was Caspar Weinberger who ended up with that plum job.

Though he didn't get the position he wanted, Bill Middendorf the composer got a decent commission in the form of the official Ronald Reagan Inauguration March. As far as I know, this was one of the spare numbered marches that was kept in the filing cabinet, but its jauntiness certainly helped to usher in what many people remember as one of the feel-good periods in America's life and times.

It's a bit of an embarrassment for me to confess that, as a card-carrying Democrat, I had a hand in celebrating the the start of the Reagan era.

At length, Bill Middendorf was appointed Ambassador to the Organization of American States. I had first known him as a diplomat; now, he was a diplomat again. Politically, he had entered a time where once again he had influence.

Musically, he had just pried open Pandora's box.

Chapter Fifteen
A Gaucho in the Kennedy Center

The Organization of American States includes dozens of countries.   From his office in Foggy Bottom, Bill was now dealing with the Colombians, the Ecuadorians, the Venezuelans, the Brazilians, an assortment of Caribbean countries — not to mention our neighour, Mexico.

Each of those countries had to be talked to, dealt with, cosseted with gifts ... and what better gift than a specially composed piece of original music?

From a composing point of view, this was like being Ambassador to the Netherlands — thirty-five times over.   Never mind that I had a burgeoning new career as a science fiction writer, and that somewhere deep inside, Other-Somtow was still attempting to break loose.

The C Street office of the ambassador was well lit and not labyrinthine like the Pentagon. I think we both realized by now that this collaboration would not go on forever. I was no longer a feckless seventeen-year-old. And Bill often seemed distracted. I did not want to pry, but years had passed since the high drama of my encounters with Isabelle. The only family member I ever saw from time to time was Frances, and she was always a welcome breath of sanity.

There were to be no long sessions in a secret closet at the State Department. What I remember most about it was that it didn't feel as secretive as the Pentagon, and there wasn't this since of grayness. Bill's inner entourage, the one that remained with him whether he was in the private sector or the government, came with him too, and Rita Fisher was again the gatekeeper.

Rita Fisher became more and more important to me, because it was she who got the cheques signed. Keeping on her good side was the most important thing in the world.

Rita was well aware of what all this music stuff meant to her boss. She knew she had to keep it running smoothly. But one thing is that as the years went by, he became more and more reluctant to pay.

I don't mean that he ever *intentionally* planned to stiff me. What it was, I think, is that had slowly come to believe that I really was a mere arranger, and that he was, in the absolute sense, the author of these

works.   The payment was a troublesome reminder
that the narrative wasn't quite true.

He had given all sorts of interviews to that effect.
His other hangers-on, the McCrackens and others, I
think, were more adept at keeping the myth alive.   I
was not entirely guiltless in this regard either; with
him, I rarely referred to any of this work as mine.
The Ted White story had been a chilling reminder
that this could be all over at any moment.

Since there was never any set fee, or any contract,
the moment of payment always felt a little awkward.
There was a tiny part of him that wondered why he
should pay at all — wasn't this his own music? — and
another part that understood how this really worked.
The moment of payment, therefore, was a little bit
weird because it brought this conflict to the fore.

Rita developed a sort of system for this.   We knew
he wouldn't sign any check until the very last minute,
and he didn't want to actually come up with an actual
figure.   So, coming up to the end of the week, she'd
ask me how much I needed, write up the check, and
slip it in amongst a bunch of other bills.

She would deliver them to him, and I'd be sitting
forlornly in an outer office.   It would seem that he
would deliberate a very long time before signing.

I have to admit that every time I received a check I
felt a twinge of humiliation.   And yet I don't think he
was ever conscious of it.

The OAS days were, in a way, a swan song, both
for Somtow-Middendorf *and* for Other-Somtow.

***

It began, I think, with Brazil.

"What can we do with Brazil?"

The meeting place of choice was usually the Army and Navy Club. But today, we were meeting at an impressive home in Washington, a home that was being lent to us by the pianist Kit Young — an important figure in the lives of both Somtows.

I have to introduce to you Kit a little, because this young pianist was a scion of the "other camp" — her father was ambassador to Thailand under John F. Kennedy, and her family were definitely Democratic Party royalty and of well-moneyed stock. The Youngs were to the left wing what the Middendorfs were to the right.

Kit spoke Thai fluently, and was always running in and out of countries like Burma, working with young people and encouraging them to elevate their lives through music. She loved to do good — and her altruism was directed at causes beloved of liberals. She was an impassioned musician — indeed, at times she even took music a little *too* seriously, preferring the sadness to the smiles. There were two things in music she seemed to love best: playing difficult modern works, and communicating the joy of music to young people.

My recollection of the house is that it was monumental. Known as "The Lindens," the house was on Kalorama Road, actually only a few blocks from the Thai Embassy. This house, built in 1745 in Massachusetts, had in fact been moved to Washington literally brick by brick in the 1930s. It was retrofitted for modern living, but made to look convincing to any time-travelling person from the 18th Century. Even the lighting fixtures were disguised to flicker with simulated candlelight.

Kit was occupying it and naturally it had a decent upright piano, and no one minded the piano being banged on at two in the morning. The piano (and the house itself) belonged to her grandmother who had had the house relocated to Washington in order to house her vast collection of early Americana.

That J. William Middendorf would even set foot in this house (you will recall that he berated me for wearing a McGovern button once, calling him the Antichrist) was a token of how high music stood in his esteem.

That such a personage could be admitted to that house was also a testament to the awesome, bipartisan power of music.

Well ... perhaps not *entirely* bipartisan.

As Kit Young later wrote to me:

> That was my grandmother's upright on which you quickened to life Middendorf's humming. And you both were sitting in the plebeian "Early American" Room with pewter ware, open fireplace and the long "settler's table" of rough-hewn pine. Upstairs was strictly for aristocrats!

As I've said, the Youngs were Democratic Party royalty. "Lower middle class intellects" were relegated to the pantry!

***

After (and in between) bouts of humming and playing, we sat and enjoyed coffee in, I think, some kind of kitchen or parlor. The room was run down yet resplendent. There were cabinets that, with a bit of a dusting or waxing, would, I knew, reveal themselves to be costly antiques. It was a blend of ostentation and shabbiness, the kind much loved in old money circles, especially liberal New England ones.

The Brazilian piece developed into a series of musical images for chamber orchestra, with a big piano part. It began softly, as though dawn were breaking. There was a movement that was supposed to be a samba, though it seemed to have elements of a tango as well. Writing for a small ensemble was nice for a change.

I wasn't at the opening and could be wrong about it but I believe that Kit Young herself played the rather virtuosic piano part. My recollection is that it might have been a concert in a museum, perhaps the Smithsonian, a daytime event.

Later, she told me, "There were all these very contemporary pieces in the program." I could imagine them well: there was a plinkety-plunk style of modern music that was really popular in academic circles. Other-Somtow was guilty of perpetuating this style himself, from time to time.

"The *Brazilian Triptych* must have really seemed out of their element," I said.

"Yeah, but here's the thing," she told me. "The audience was suffering bravely through all that avant-garde music. But as soon as the Middendorf began, there was a palpable sigh of relief. It's like they were all thinking, *At last! Proper music!*"

Bill Middendorf really understood his audience.

***

There followed a series of works inspired by different Latin American countries. The *Fantasias de Maracaibo,* the *Mexican Rhapsody, and* the piece for Trinidadian steel drums. Marches were put on hold.

***

One of the amazing things about my time in Washington post-Bangkok intermezzo was that people who were fixtures of my time in Bangkok had started to resurface in America. One of these was Kit Young. Another was the polymath and bon vivant, Bob Halliday.

To my amazement, Bob had surfaced in Washington and was working in a bookstore — not an ordinary bookstore but a discount place specializing in remainders, those leftover hardcovers that publishers sell off cheap when they want to put a book out of print.

Whenever his friends would visit, Bob would give away selected hardcovers, often books that would have cost a fortune were they not remaindered. I often left with entire tote bags full. It was amazing to me that he had not been summarily dismissed.

But in this bookstore, Bob held court; all the dispossessed intellectuals flocked to him as their guru. It was through Bob that I meant some of the most influential people in the city, like Mike Dirda, who would later win the Pulitzer Prize, but who ran the Washington *Post* book review section and had the power of life and death over careers such as mine, because he could assign reviews to anyone he chose.

I was very fortunate to have some of my early novels reviewed in the *Post* by such people as Orson

Scott Card (author of *Ender's Game)* or Theodore Sturgeon, one of the most influential science fiction writers of the Golden Age. As my writing became more established and as I made more appearances at conventions, I came to know more or less every luminary in the field, from the "big" authors like Isaac Asimov and Robert Heinlein all the way down to people who were starting out at the same time as me, like William Gibson or Orson Scott Card. By now, I was also Membership Chairman, then Secretary, of the Science Fiction Writers of America — though years later I was called "the worst SFWA Secretary of all time" by no less a figure than Jerry Pournelle.

These people were to come in really handy when I came to try, for the third time, to immigrate to the United States, where I was, but for the saving grace of a diplomatic passport, technically an illegal alien marked for deportation.

***

As long as there remained Latin American countries to inspire rhapsodies, nocturnes and the like, however, my uneasy foothold in America remained extant.

One of the most visible pieces I did for the OAS countries was the *Fantasias de Maracaibo,* for piano and orchestra, which was performed at the Kennedy Center by the National Symphony Orchestra, I believe in honour of some important diplomatic occasion between the U.S. and Venezuela.

This was a pleasant, but not especially brilliant piece of music that had, as the pianist said, "a really nice Spanish kind of flavor." I was despatched by Bill Middendorf to listen in on the rehearsal and keep an eye on things. The pianist said some very kind things about the piece. But, there was this huge romantic melody and to my horror, I noticed that at its climax, I had accidentally (excuse the pun) forgotten to put in a natural sign on the bass note. This resulted in a crashing, resounding discord at the moment that should have been most moving.

I waited for the next break and said to the conductor, "Sorry, maestro, but that note is supposed to be a B flat — could you just change it?"

The conductor looked at me — still pretty much a kid and with very unpresentable attire and hair — and looked right through me. When I repeated myself, he simply said, "How would you know? Who the hell are you?"

I slunk away.

What was I to do, tell him I'd written the piece? Why would the National Symphony be deigning to play it at all if it weren't composed by an ambassador? What the hell was I doing there indeed? He had hit the nail on the head: for in this world of illusions, I was truly nobody at all.

The Washington *Post* was not very kind to poor Bill's piece.

> The evening was also the occasion of the world premiere of "Fantasy for Maracaibo" by J. William Middendorf. It was forgettable schlock, a waste of good musicianship. The Maracaibo Symphony must have had its reasons to play this work by Middendorf, who happens to be the U.S. ambassador to the Organization of American States. But these could not have been artistic.

One could say, therefore, that there were certain advantages to being no one. This piece was pretty forgettable, yet it was pleasant enough, and would have been a delightful opus number in the catalogue of some minor nineteenth century composer. It probably didn't deserve to be so cruelly attacked. Perhaps there was a political motive — Bill would certainly have assumed so. However, being in the same program as De Falla, Tchaikovsky and Bartok probably didn't help.

We were still a few years from the revelations of the Iran-Contra scandal.

***

Dingwall Fleary perhaps took pity on me, for he suggested that I write something for the McLean Symphony — something of my own.

Star Maker: An Anthology of Universes was to be Other-Somtow's bid for independent fame in the American musical universe, and I wrote the piece with all the technical ambition I could dredge up.

Each movement of the piece was based on a different theory of the universe, with titles like *Big Bang: the Cyclical Universe, The Platonic Universe,* the *Ptolemaic Universe,* and *Inferno, Purgatorio, Paradiso.*

The McLean Symphony's horns were not, at the time, very good — I had learned that to my cost on the Middendorf Seventh — so I simply left them out of this work. The orchestra's bassoonist, Joel Eigen, had remarkably also learned to play the shakuhachi, the seductive Japanese flute that has a huge repertoire of sounds, shrieking, sobbing, gliding, and throbbing.

This was therefore going to be the first piece in history that called for bassoon doubling shakuhachi.

Kit Young bashing through the piano part of Star Maker: An Anthology of Universes

I also used a number of Orff metallophones, very resonant instruments used to teach children in the Carl Orff educational system.   I had these instruments, which I was paying for in installments; the large one was in daily use in my living room — as a coffee table. A children's chorus was recruited to do everything *except* sing — whispering, screaming, shouting and so on.

The movements actually *were* based on the theories of the universe they were named after — these were not just fanciful names. For example, the Big Bang movement began and ended with a musical

Big Bang. The entire movement was a palindrome (suggesting that the universe would expand and then contract back into a singularity) and each of the instrumental parts was also a series of interlocking palindromes. Yes, it was pretty wild.

There was a review in one Northern Virginia paper which was complimentary but a little baffled.

Despite the bafflement, the intrepid Dingwall Fleary revived my piece a couple of years later, with an extra movement added. In my files, I have only managed to locate three of the movements.

***

In the buildup to the Iran-Contra scandal, Bill Middendorf's catalogue of OAS-related pieces grew. My own introduction to the scandal occurred when, one day, I drove down to a tiny little Chinese restaurant in Alexandria whose food I enjoyed immensely.

However, I couldn't get in. Secret servicemen were walking around and several large black cars blocked me from entering. An hour later, I went in to see everything as normal.

I asked Sam Chan what was going on.

"Oh, my old boss come to get favorite food," he said.

"Your old boss?"

"Yes, Bill Casey."

I had just missed the head of the CIA. Apparently he would come to Po Sam's restaurant whenever needed comfort food; Sam had worked for him for years, but had left and started his own business.

Sam was one of the most interesting restauranteers I ever knew. He had the best stories — like having to sauté human livers during the war, or running around the house with a hatchet, trying to kill an escaped suckling pig.

He didn't tell me whether these exotic dishes were part of Bill Casey's "comfort food", but I knew that the craving for comfort food tends to be a result of extreme stress.

For Iran-Contra was about to start dominating the news cycles.

CHAPTER SIXTEEN
A BURNOUT IN ALEXANDRIA

The Indian summer of our collaboration was to last only a little bit longer.

There were a total of nineteen OAS-related pieces, according to a note I have here. I know this is possible, because there are 35 countries in the OAS, but to be honest, I don't remember them all. I certainly don't remember Nicaragua being among the countries celebrated in Bill Middendorf's work, but then again maybe there was too much *other* stuff going on with Nicaragua to have any time left for musical endeavors.

It was during the the Iran-Contra incident that the moment in the elevator occurred, the one with which I began this memoir.

We had been working in the Army and Navy Club. Usually this would be late at night, but I had less time now for these five-hour sessions. I don't know why I was in the elevator by myself.

I don't remember what we had composed that evening. Perhaps it was the march for Belizian independence. One event in those sessions was very strange: it was when he suggested it might be fun to have a piece that was just like Beethoven's Fifth, except that instead if starting da-da-da-DUM ... it would go da-da-da-da-DUM. Just one extra note.

"Think we could get away with it?" he had said, with a mischievous giggle.

I remember that later that evening Bill took me into a lobby area where various people sitting on couches, some nursing drinks. At one of these couches, Oliver North was sitting, looking very despondent. I recognized him from the live television hearings.

Bill Middendorf asked him how he was bearing up and he sort of shrugged and had a faraway look. Bill introduced me, but he didn't say anything.

"It's terrible," Bill told me later, "what they're making him go through...."

***

Among the last things we created, as I recall, were some virtuoso compositions for piano and orchestra. Part of this came from meeting Alan Mandel, specialist in Scott Joplin and Louis Gottschalk, and one of the best known American pianists. He was charming to Bill, and asked him for a piano concerto.

We soon started working on one, somewhat Rachmaninovian in its melodies and harmonies.

We showed it to Alan and he professed to be quite pleased.

Later, he got me by myself and asked me to tell him what was really going on. I hemmed and hawed, but he more or less figured it out.

Not in all its complexities, however. What he seemed to have figured out was that there might be money to be had here.

He also told me that the concerto needed to be a harder to play. "I can't play something like this in public unless it's *really* difficult. That will get the piece respect. Please, make it a lot more difficult than this."

He then asked me how much I thought he could charge. "Just give me a ballpark figure," he said. "I'll need to be well paid. How much should I ask for?"

This was a rather complex dynamic for me to deal with. It was clear that Mandel wasn't making inquiries out of respect for Bill Middendorf as a musician. He also figured I could do up something to order. He could kill several birds with one stone: have a piece of impressive virtuosity written just for him, derive some political advantage from the piece's author, and make money.

I couldn't really answer his question because by then I knew that my primary motivation wasn't making money. I say this even though I did need the money to survive.

Adding to the oeuvre of J. William Middendorf, II, wasn't just a job for me. It was an addiction.

Cold turkey was going to be the only solution.

I did in fact ending producing a piano concerto —
a rather Russian-sounding one as I recall.   I also
started in earnest to revive my quest to have some
kind of recognizable legal status in America.

from the Middendorf Variations for piano and
orchestra, *my handwriting*

It turned out that the key to a green card was not through the influence of people in high places. In the end, it was about money.

From time to time, my father as a diplomat had to attend the U.N. General Assembly in New York, and my parents would rent an apartment on Bleecker Street from an old friend named Rasri Pratoomas, who worked in a law firm in New York that often did immigration cases.

I didn't think that I could get back on the treadmill; after all, I'd already been rejected, and I didn't know whether one could appeal such things. I didn't think that there was that much interest from Bill Middendorf in straightening out my status. After all, I was in a very useful state of dependency, being unable to get a "normal" sort of job.

Rasri introduced me to a lawyer who said, "Well, this is an open and shut case. I can arrange it for $3,000. I promise you, that is a cheap price to pay for not having to deal with those people — when they see *me,* it's a familiar face. It will go quickly."

It wasn't so much that there was collusion and cronyism between the lawyers and the INS. It was more a question of knowing everyone on the inside, feeling comfortable with each other, and under-standing exactly what these bureaucrats wanted. The method I had tried before, the "third preference" visa, was the right one, but I had not gone about it right.

"First," he said, "you needed to overwhelm them with evidence. Boxes and boxes of books, magazines, and clippings showing that you are God's gift to America."

After that, he said, came the most important thing

— letters from celebs.

"You probably think that glowing encomiums are the way to go, but they're not," he said.   "They actually go through the letters and look for two key phrases.   If they find those two phrases, the letter passes muster.   I know you know a lot of great writers, but let's not try to get too creative here.   The two phrases are 'extraordinary ability' and 'distinguished merit.'   They can say anything they like, but the first paragraph has to say who they are, and the recommendation must contain those two phrases.   Now, get me at least fifty of those."

I wrote to many of friends and they in turn wrote me back.   Those who spent the longest time on the first paragraph, which revealed who they are, were generally less famous than those who dismissed their own credentials in a single sentence.

For example. Catherine Crook De Camp, a distinguished writer but perhaps not that famous, attached her entire resume plus a xerox of her entry in the *Authors and Writers Who's Who*.   Isaac Asimov, on the other hand, had a very short first paragraph, which began "I, Isaac Asimov...."   The recommendation itself said, "He has shown extraordinary ability and distinguished merit."   Isaac Asimov didn't fuck around.

My lawyer put the Asimov letter on the top of the heap, took my passport, and in short order got a little rubber stamp in it that meant my application had been successfully submitted.

It had taken six years to *not* get the application past the counter, and a week or two for a lawyer to do so.

"Actually," he told me, "they only looked at the Asimov letter. But it was important to have the entire pile. The look is the thing."

Today he would have used the word "optics", but that expression in that meaning was not yet in use in the 1980s.

***

Since *Star Maker,* I had tried to start a new opera (I mean, my Other had) several times. Most recently, I had begun an operatic adaptation of Gene Wolfe's lauded novella, *The Death of Dr. Island,* which a libretto by the author of the original book.

The idea was to have it performed in Australia, where Gene Wolfe was to be the Guest of Honor at the World Science Fiction Convention in 1985.

Interestingly, the opera showed clearly that I was moving in a different direction. Though it was colorfully orchestrated as Other-Somtow's previous works, in was moving towards — the horror — *tonality.*

In my student years, that was a giant no-no. To say new things, one turned to the musical language of one's immediate antecedents — Stockhausen, or Boulez — or else one risked ridicule by one's peers, or accusations of being a sellout.

In a sense, the entire Middendorfian adventure had been, for me, a guilty pleasure — an excuse to deploy the tropes of romanticism without being accused of letting down the side.

Now, the opening number of this opera, which set to music Gene Wolfe's epigraph — worlds by Gerard Manley Hopkins — had the music going through a cycle, beginning with sheer atonality and then filtering it down to a big, unmistakeable, climactic D major chord ... three times. A big fat bit of tonality trying to assert itself through the white noise.

Perhaps it was the shock that a third composing persona was attempting to be born that drove me to burn out.

But yes, it happened. One morning, I found myself completely bereft of notes. Nothing came out.

The third Somtow was too scary to exist.

Writing science fiction was a lot safer.

***

Shortly after that, I received word that my green card had come through, and that I should go up to New York to receive it.

***

What now?

I was the lucky recipient of what is often referred to as the "genius visa." I did not feel in the slightest bit genius-like, however. I had spent a heady eighteen months in Thailand trying to "revolutionize all art" and been soundly beaten down by the establishment. I had composed almost two hundred pieces of music under someone else's name, music of which only intermittent fragments made me feel I had any talent.

At the moment, it was only the writing that gave me any sense of self-esteem. And science fiction was still a niche market, relegated to its own section in the bookstore, in the back, away from the "real" books out front.

The "genius visa" did give me something very

important, however. It gave me my freedom.

I wasn't dependent on anyone's largesse. If I ran out of money, I could flip burgers or make slurpies at 7-11. There were wide open spaces to conquer. There were new dreams to dream.

I was still young enough to reinvent myself.

Thus it was that I ended up doing what Huckleberry Finn did — the thing that one does that is quintessentially American.

I went to IKEA and bought a U-Haul's worth of flat furniture, and, with little fuss, I "lit out for the territory." I said goodbye to no one, least of all to the person who had, one way or another, dominated my existence for more than a dozen years.

at the recording of the Holland Symphony

CHAPTER SEVENTEEN
A JOURNEY TO THE WEST

Unlike in novels — I know this because I've written over fifty of them — real life doesn't tie itself neatly off, doesn't split into exact chapters.

But my journey to California sure felt like a novelistic cut off point.

Other-Somtow had gone silent.

Somtow-cum-Middendorf had been petering out, and now that flame, too, seemed spent.

Because I don't like to give complicated answers, I usually tell interviewers or casual acquaintances that it was the failure of the Bangkok revolution that made me burn out, but it was a little more complicated than that.

I wanted to tell myself that Other-Somtow was the "real" composer, the avant-garde revolutionary, fighting off the reactionaries. In that world-view, the Somtow who dashed off marches was a necessary evil, prostituting his abilities to subsdize the "real" composer and investing nothing of himself in the work at all.

But there was an uncomfortable truth hidden in there. Much as I believed I was catering to a middle-aged millionaire's dream, a facilitator, not a creator, there was also a part of Somtow that yearned to be Middendorf.

What I mean by that is I wanted to be someone who could feel no guilt or peer pressure at pumping out big fat romantic tunes and lush harmonies.

So, did J. William Middendorf, II, disappear from my life the minute I set foot in California?

Pretty much. The problem is that *both* Somtows were gone. What now emerged was a brand new persona: S.P. Somtow, the "Terrifying Thai."

Science fiction, written at first as a therapeutic exercise, had become the dominant percentage of my income even before leaving the east coast. Those books were at first published under the name Somtow Sucharitkul. It was an exotic name — there really weren't any Asian science fiction writers yet, though many were to follow — and science fiction readers didn't mind alien-sounding names.

But when I wanted to write something that could appeal to a larger audience, the novel *Vampire Junction,* I had some difficulty selling it. All in all it was rejected by some thirty publishers. One reason was that it was outrageous and over-the-top in terms of sex and violence, yet dared to have literary pretensions.

Eventually, three editors who had *wanted* to buy the rights to this book when they were working at different publishers, but had been nixed by their superiors — Beth Meacham, Susan Allison, and Ginjer Buchanan — all ended up at Ace/Berkley — and they managed to overrule their boss, working in concert — as long as changed my name to something (and I quote, so please don't be offended) "that rednecks in Georgia can pronounce." This is how S.P. was born. But S.P. eventually took over my writing career, and when the old science fiction titles were reprinted, lo and behold! S.P. had written those as well. Soon S.P. wasn't a science fiction writer at all; he was an all-purpose novelist with horror novels, historical novels, a *bildungsroman* called *Jasmine Nights* that made London's *Observer* newspaper's *Best of the Year* list ...then branching out to being a director of two obscure films, a writer of animation scripts including an episode of *Chip 'n' Dale's Rescue Rangers,* and even a satirical B-movie for Roger Corman.

S.P.'s burgeoning career overshadowed his entire past. I never thought of returning to ghost-writing symphonies, nor did I think I would ever return to Thailand to be a flaming revolutionary. Thoughts of creating music faded from my mind. I would go to concerts and enjoy them without any feeling that I was myself a professional musician. The transformation seemed to have happened overnight.

By the time I picked up music again, I was in a completely different place. I needed a soundtrack for a B-movie called *The Laughing Dead* which I had cooked up with the financial help of Lex Nakashima, a Japanese-American science fiction fan. This tragicomic extravaganza starred mostly amateurs who in real life were actually science fiction writers.

A decade had passed. Something called the MIDI revolution had occurred while I was away from music, which enabled me to create an entire symphony orchestra, backup choir and any number of exotic instruments entirely on a computer in my sleazily genteel hovel in a rather slummy L.A. neighborhood. The voice I wrote in was a new one. Film music liberated me from the idea that I'd be excoriated by my peers for not being modern enough — yet allowed me to be as modern-sounding as I wanted when the images were appropriate — a monster, a dream sequence, a serial killer, or the like.

But since I was now a novelist, not a composer, I only did film music occasionally — usually it was for some low-budget thing where some director would ask me to "save the bad acting" by overwhelming it with a bombastic score, and I'd pick up a quick ten grand for a week's work.

I didn't escape the Republican party right away. How could I, when I had been embedded so long — even, in a sense, suffered from Stockholm syndrome? Once I became a citizen, though, I started voting for the blues.

But I got flashbacks. When I saw a youtube video of Sarah Palin exorcising witches, my mind raced right back to Isabelle Middendorf in the house in McLean.

By the mid-nineties, someone in Thailand remembered my existence and I would occasionally be invited back to conduct something or other.

By 2001, I had fulfilled a long-nurtured dream — producing my own opera — in Bangkok.

In all of those years, J. William Middendorf, II, did not seem to surface at all. It was another life, another world. I did from time to time hear news from the east coast. But his compositional career also seems to have dribbled to a halt. I suppose he never found another amanuensis who truly understood where he was coming from.

Recently, I read a book he had written about his experiences in the political universe of Washington.

He does mention me in it. It's complimentary, although it skirts the issue of what I *actually* did for him.

***

At length, something happened that would wrench my life down a completely different path; as I was driving down the Pacific Coast Highway from San Francisco, I was overcome by an irresistible urge to enter a Buddhist monastery.

I called my travel agent and I was on a plane the next day to Bangkok. In a matter of days, I was shaved, wearing a saffron robe, and entering a deep meditative state.

But *that* adventure must be the subject of a separate book. Which book, *Nirvana Express,* you can buy as well, if you've enjoyed this one.

Chapter Eighteen
A Lesson in Mythmaking

I'm 65 years old now, and I'm looking back at this incredible adventure that started when I was 17 and devoured a decade and a half of my life.

I've dined out on many of the anecdotes that I've now strung together to form this memoir. But now it's time to put it all together. I never signed any non-disclosure agreement, after all, and it is a tale worth telling, with more twists and turns than fiction, with fascinating and eccentric characters ... and writing it has also been a kind of exorcism, a more successful one than the one Mrs. Middendorf once tried out on Christmas morning, so long ago.

But there is one question that haunts me, and that I am only now confronting. It's a question of identity.

This composer named J. William Middendorf, the Second — *who was he?*

Was he me? After all, I wrote 99% of the notes of this composer's oeuvre. I took germs of ideas, or inchoate humming, and teased them into acceptable pastiches of music from another era. I have over a decade of inkstained fingers to show it was me, because this was all before the time when computers made our jobs so much easier.

Or was he *him?* Those fragmentary snatches of humming were definitely his own. And I was paid — indeed, well paid. Later when I worked for literary franchises, or when I wrote scripts for cartoons like *Chip 'n' Dale's Rescue Ranges,* I learned that this was legally *work for hire.* The copyright on my cartoon script belongs to Disney. I am legally in no way its owner.

Since I was paid, quite well at times, and it was understood that I would forgo any co-writing credit, it would certainly be legitimate to opine that Bill Middendorf was the sole composer.

Publicly at least, for four decades, I've stuck to the official tale because I myself didn't want to be seen as a creator of this retro music, this half-remembered homage to romanticism.

And yet....

Though I didn't originate it, I did egg him on. Though some melodic snatches are identifiably his, the notes are in my hand. Though secretly I sometimes felt embarrassed, openly I often felt pride.

Though as a "high-minded artist" I would act as though I disdained the "filthy lucre" aspects of the relationship, I was really glad of the money, and felt that it validated my abilities.

I wanted to share this narrative because one day some enterprising journalist, like Ted White, thirty years ago, will uncover some nuggets of this story and will connect the dots to form a shallower narrative.

Perhaps someone who despises Republicans would fashion a tale of an evil man exploiting an Asian boy and passing off other people's art as his own — and blame it all on a "vast right-wing conspiracy." Which is not true at all. Bill was and is a prominent Republican and believes in their agenda and values, but he was never a demagogue. He could see more than one viewpoint, and was often discomfited by extremism amongst his own tribe.

Then again, someone who views Asians as mercenary exploiter, raping western civilization, might view this as the story of how a sneaky Asian boy hoodwinked a wannabe composer and flattered him into parting with his dough.

Either way, it would be positioned as tale of people taking advantage of each other and weaving a tapestry of mendacities, putting one over on each other and the outside world.

In the final third of my life, I've come to realize how much more J. William Middendorf, II, was to me than a benefactor, father figure, and meal ticket.

In the ten years or so that I completely gave up music, the two personae I had buried deep in my unconscious seem to have come to an understanding. Because the composer who emerged after being silenced for a decade was neither of the two composers I had repressed.

There are qualities in the music I write now — which *does* get real reviews and real respect from critics and peers, most of the time — that clearly show the influence of Bill Middendorf.

I'm no longer scared of the past. I learned to compose music I *want* to compose, not music I *ought* to compose.

I learned that it's perfectly cool to use *every* musical language that one has absorbed during one's creative journey — whether it's romanticism or atonality, Asian or western — and that is a lesson I learned from J. William Middendorf, II.

I've learned to have faith in my musical vision no matter how personal it seems; and to ignore critics and naysayers — yes, also a lesson from Bill.

Thanks to having to write endless orchestral works and actually getting them performed by proper orchestras, I *really* learned, in the most practical way possible, how to orchestrate. Bill Middendorf made it possible.

I got a worm's eye view of places of power and privilege I would never otherwise have witnessed, perspectives that served me well in writing fiction set in other worlds.

I admit to more than a twinge of envy that these notes I'd painstakingly written out were being played at the Kennedy Center, by orchestras like the St. Louis Symphony, the Boston Pops, and the National Symphony. without my name on them. But forty years later, having conducted Mahler in Berlin and had my works played in Carnegie Hall and

Musikverein in Vienna and so on, those turbulent feelings are gone.

And I am finally able to acknowledge this truth: that J. William Middendorf's influence permeates every-thing I do.

And on the whole, despite periods of trauma and self-doubt, I'm the better for it.

So, who *wrote* Bill Middendorf's music?

***

There was a moment when our identities almost converged.   That was during the creation of the opera, *The Lion and the Rose.*

In an article in the *Standard-Times,* an interviewer notes that the opera "is yet to be performed. Mr. Middendorf knows why. 'It's three hours long,' the composer says. "Who wants to put on an opera that long?'"

That, too, is my biggest regret.   *The Lion and the Rose* was an ambitious work that certain contains moments that come close to true epic.   One of my friends from Alexandria, Gus Edwards, said of the recorded excerpts, "My God — it's an opera consisting entirely of climaxes!"

The thing is, I now have an opera company. Perhaps, if enough interest is aroused by this book, I'll event mount the opera.   It's a curiosity, but it's tuneful and more "operatic" than most operas.

The Lion and Rose is as close as I ever came to *wanting* to take credit for this collaboration.   I poured all my operatic fantasies into it.   I would also say that this opera contains the smallest percentage of thematic material that actually originated from Bill. And yet — in its subject matter, its wildly Hollywood-epic vision of history, its swashbuckling sense of adventure — it was very much part and parcel of Bill's esthetic.

***

Bill also showed me I had a lot to learn about mythmaking. Compared to him, I was, and am, a rank amateur.

In a review of one of my galaxy-spanning space operas, a critic called me "a mythmaker". But in terms of practical mythmaking, Bill Middendorf was the master.

Talking to the press, he created a homespun, plain-speaking and self-deprecating image of himself, as witness this quote from the Chicago *Tribune:*

> "It's really not much different than laying bricks," Middendorf says in a modest way. "There is a discipline in bricklaying — and in the other arts and crafts."

Disarming, charming, and cunningly defanging potential critics. Here's another choice quote, from the Boston *Globe:*

> "It's getting easier to write music, the secretary says, "but it is still hard. I'm just glad I don't make as many mistakes as I did at the beginning."

I agree. In many of these newspaper articles, I'm mentioned. It's always complimentary and always gracious. Bill always went out of his way to mention me.   Usually it says that I was a promising young student who tutored him. Not untrue.

> "I play the piano. I'll hear a tune in my head and sit down and work it out. I leave the subtleties to someone else."

That's a quote from the *Evening Sun*. It's almost true. The only statement that flirts with untruth is the actual point in the process in which "someone else" showed up ... who actually "sat down and worked it out."

And his conducting! What does *South Coast Today* say?

> People tell him he's not very good at it. And he agrees. "I'm awkward," I says, "and stiff. But let me tell you something. It sure is a nice little ego trip."

Adorable!   No matter that he misses the entire point of what a conductor does — that is to say, interpret, leading the audience toward deeper and deeper levels of undiscovered meaning.   Wilhelm Fürtwängler was awkward — he just happened to be the greatest conductor of his generation.

So, you see, Bill Middendorf created a lovable persona, a bumbling. avuncular, jovial gentleman who somehow, puttering around here and there, just happened to come up with these symphonies and marches. I believe that on some level, he believed it. He did not consider what we did in secret to be dishonest.

After all, Bill had taken some sketches and had them made into a stained glass window, and felt no discrepancy when he told people he "made" the stained glass window. He also once created a likeness of his wife in clay, and had someone turn it into a bronze sculpture.

On some level, he believed that what we did was a kind of variation of the same process.

The difference is really this: Bill *was* an accomplished artist. Not only did have art school training and understand the techniques involved, but he had a genuine artistic vision in the visual arts; his drawing and paintings have a recognizable, consistent style. When you looked at the sketch of the stained glass window, and then saw the actual window, they were recognizably the same work.

This really could not be said if you were to compare a snatch of humming to a movement of a symphony.

And yet … it was he who provided the spark, the central vision.

There's a German word that I usually have to explicate a bit when I teach my students about romanticism. This word is *Sehnsucht*.

It's absolutely central to romanticism in music, and the word is usually translated as "longing". But it is so much more than that.

Sehnsucht is the kind of longing that totally possess you, a longing for that which is unattainable, a longing one is willing to die for, indeed for which the only possible consummation is death.

When Bill Middendorf hummed an inchoate germ of a melody to me, his whole pysche was permeated with *Sehnsucht*.

He just lit up. His passion was undeniable. It was

a infectious. It was completely convincing because it was completely real.

"I leave the subtleties to someone else." In Bill's case, the "subtleties" generally included 99% of the actual notes. But the 1% came from *Sehnsucht*. The longing. The passion to intersect with something greater than oneself. The yearning to experience a shadow of divinity.

Bill was a fine artist, a canny businessman, a resourceful politician, and successful diplomat. He had struggled to climb, had conquered and reached the summit of those endeavoured. But the summit he truly wanted was the summit he could not attain. And on some level he knew this. He was Tantalus, the always grasping at the fruit that hung just beyond his reach. That was what drove the passion.

The most important thing I learned from Bill Middendorf is that you *must* have this passion. Without it, an artist has nothing. I took this passion and I dressed it as best I could, clumsily at first and later with greater and greater self-assurance. But the spark was his alone. He was the one who dreamed it.

It's for this reason that if I were now answer the question, "Who wrote Bill Middendorf's music?" I would have to answer, in all honesty, J. William Middendorf, II, wrote it.

I wrote this memoir, in part, because I was searching for an answer to this question.

In looking back at these events, I've found more to admire than to deprecate in this larger-than-life personality. In the past, there were times I thought that he had deflected me from my true path, even, in a sense, robbed me of my childhood. There were moments when I despised him, wondering how he could create those myths with a straight face.

Now, though, I've come to understand him. Because I learned from him to find my own passion, my own vision. The long deflection was no detour at all. It was a necessary, lengthy and painful schooling in what it means to be an artist.

It has been a life-changing lesson to be the tinkling cymbal to his sounding brass.

For this lesson, Bill Middendorf will always have my gratitude, and my love.

About the Author

Once referred to by the International Herald Tribune as "the most well-known expatriate Thai in the world," Somtow Sucharitkul is no longer an expatriate, since he has returned to Thailand after five decades of wandering the world. He is best known as an award-winning novelist and a composer of operas.

Born in Bangkok, Somtow grew up in Europe and was educated at Eton and Cambridge. His first career was in music and in the 1970s he acquired a reputation as a revolutionary composer, the first to combine Thai and Western instruments in radical new sonorities. Conditions in the arts in the region at the time proved so traumatic for the young composer that he suffered a major burnout, emigrated to the United States, and reinvented himself as a novelist.

His earliest novels were in the science fiction field but he soon began to cross into other genres. In his 1984 novel *Vampire Junction,* he injected a new literary inventiveness into the horror genre, in the words of Robert Bloch, author of *Psycho,* "skilfully combining the styles of Stephen King, William Burroughs, and the author of the Revelation to John." *Vampire Junction* was voted one of the forty all-time greatest horror books by the Horror Writers' Association, joining established classics like *Frankenstein* and *Dracula*.

In the 1990s Somtow became increasingly identified as a uniquely Asian writer with novels such as the semi-autobiographical Jasmine Nights. He won the World Fantasy Award, the highest accolade given in the world of fantastic literature, for his novella *The Bird Catcher.* His fifty-three books have sold about two million copies world-wide.After becoming a Buddhist monk for a period in 2001, Somtow decided to refocus his attention on the country of his birth, founding Bangkok's first international opera company and returning to music, where he again reinvented himself, this time as a neo-Asian neo-Romantic composer. The Norwegian government commissioned his song cycle *Songs Before Dawn* for the 100th Anniversary of the Nobel Peace Prize, and he composed at the request of the government of Thailand his *Requiem: In Memoriam 9/11* which was dedicated to the victims of the 9/11 tragedy.

According to London's Opera magazine, "in just five years, Somtow has made Bangkok into the operatic hub of Southeast Asia." His operas on Thai themes, *Madana, Mae Naak, Ayodhya*, and *The Silent Prince* have been well received by international critics. His most recent operas, the Japanese inspired *Dan no Ura* and the fantasy opera *The Snow Dragon,* have gained him acceptance as "one of the most intriguing of contemporary opera com-posers" (Auditorium Magazine). He has recently embarked on a ten-opera cycle, *Dasjati — Ten Lives of the Buddha* - which when completed will be the classical music work with the largest time span and scope in history.

He is increasingly in demand as a conductor specializing in opera and in the late-romantic composers like Mahler. His repertoire runs the entire gamut from Monteverdi to Wagner. His work has been especially lauded for its stylistic authenticity and its lyricism. He has received the "Golden W" from the International Wagner Society. The orchestra he founded in Bangkok, the Siam Philharmonic, mounted the first complete Mahler cycle in the region.

Somtow's current project, the Siam Sinfonietta, is a youth orchestra he founded five years ago, using a new educational method he pioneered and which is now among the most acclaimed youth orchestras world-wide, receiving standing ovations in Carnegie Hall, The Konzerthaus in Berlin, Disney Hall, the Musikverein in Vienna, and many other venues around the world.

He is the first recipient of Thailand's "Distin-guished Silpathorn" award, given for an artist who has made and continues to make a major impact on the region's culture, from Thailand's Ministry of Culture.

He is the first Asian (and only the second composer after Hans Werner Henze) to receive the Europa Kultur-Forum's European Cultural Achieve-ment Award.

Books by S.P. Somtow

General Fiction
The Shattered Horse
Jasmine Nights
Forgetting Places
The Other City of Angels (Bluebeard's Castle)
The Stone Buddha's Tears

Dark Fantasy
The Timmy Valentine Series:
    Vampire Junction
    Valentine
    Vanitas
Vampire Junction Special Edition
Moon Dance
Darker Angels
The Vampire's Beautiful Daughter

Science Fiction
Starship & Haiku

Mallworld
The Ultimate Mallworld
The Ultimate, Ultimate, Ultimate Mallworld
Chronicles of the High Inquest:
    Light on the Sound
    The Darkling Wind
    The Throne of Madness
    Utopia Hunters
Chroniques de l'Inquisition - Volume 1 (omnibus)
Chroniques de l'Inquisition - Volume 2 (omnibus)
Inquestor Tales One: The Singing Moons

The Aquiliad Series:
    Aquila in the New World
    Aquila and the Iron Horse
    Aquila and the Sphinx

Fantasy
The Riverrun Trilogy:
    Riverrun
    Armorica
    Yestern
The Riverrun Trilogy (omnibus)
The Fallen Country
Wizard's Apprentice
The Snow Dragon (omnibus)

Media Tie-in
The Alien Swordmaster
Symphony of Terror
The Crow - Temple of Night
Star Trek: Do Comets Dream?

Chapbooks
Fiddling for Waterbuffaloes
I Wake from a Dream of a Drowned Star City
A Lap Dance with the Lobster Lady
Compassion — Two Perspectives

Libretti
Mae Naak
Ayodhya
Madana
Dan no Ura
Helena Citronova
The Snow Dragon
Dasjati:
> *Temiya - The Silent Prince*
> *Sama - The Faithful Son*
> *Bhuridat - The Dragon Lord*
> *Mahosadha - Architect of Dreams*
> *Nemiraj - Chariot of Heaven*

Collections
My Cold Mad Father (in press)
Fire from the Wine Dark Sea
Chui Chai (Thai)
Nova (Thai)
The Pavilion of Frozen Women
Dragon's Fin Soup
Tagging the Moon
Face of Death (Thai)
Other Edens
S.P. Somtow's The Great Tales (Thai)
Terror Nova (in press)

Terror Antiqua (in press)

Essays, Poetry and Miscellanies
Opus Fifty
A Certain Slant of "I" (in press)
Sonnets about Serial Killers
Opera East
Victory in Vienna (ed.)
Three Continents (ed.)
Nirvana Express
Caravaggio x 2
The Maestro's Noctuary

www.ingramcontent.com/pod-product-compliance
Lightning Source LLC
Chambersburg PA
CBHW031838090426
42741CB00005B/277